The Team Process

A Handbook for Teachers

Third and Expanded Edition

ELLIOT Y. MERENBLOOM

National Middle School Association

NMSA

Elliot Y. Merenbloom is Director of Middle School Instruction for the Baltimore County (Maryland) Public Schools. He rose to prominence as the successful principal of the Pikesville Middle School in Baltimore County. Long active in the cause of middle level education, he has conducted highly regarded institutes and workshops on teaming, scheduling, and other aspects of middle level education all across the country.

This volume represents the second major expansion of this handbook originally published in 1983. The Association is most grateful to Elliot for his willingness to prepare this latest contribution to our Association and to the middle school movement.

Copyright © 1991 by National Middle School Association
2600 Corporate Exchange Drive, Suite 370, Columbus, OH 43231-1672

Sixth Printing, August 1996

ISBN: 1-56090-054-7

ii

Contents

Foreword

Few educators would take issue with the contention that a preferred way to organize a middle school faculty is by teams. Some would even go so far as to say it is the only way. Although status studies have shown that departmentalization still predominates, the use of teams is generally accepted among middle level educators as the better way to organize. More and more schools are implementing teaming every year, and there is hardly a middle level school in existence that is not giving consideration to its use.

Unfortunately, believing in the validity of teaming and putting it into practice are two different things. Most middle level teachers have had no specific preparation for working in teams or in interrelating subjects. They need help in order to implement this desirable arrangement. And such help cannot be provided in one or two quick, easy lessons.

This monograph, however, offers the kind of assistance needed by faculties serious about the business of interdisciplinary instruction and improving their service to students. It is thorough, practical, reality based, and field tested. Sufficiently detailed and replete with examples, it is appropriately called a handbook for it is designed for hands-on use rather than as a treatise simply to be read.

The Team Process: A Handbook for Teachers has long been a best seller. First published in 1983, it was reprinted many times to meet demand. Merenbloom then graciously volunteered to do a second and expanded edition which was published in 1986. It, too, went through several reprintings because the handbook continued to meet a real need among middle level faculties. Now comes the third and still further expanded edition of this stalwart monograph.

New materials have been added and revisions in original materials have been made as a result of extensive use with teachers and administrators in the field. What has resulted is a still more comprehensive handbook, one that in previous editions already proved its mettle. This edition will extend the reputation of *The Team Process: A Handbook for Teachers* and insure its value in advancing more integrated instruction.

John H. Lounsbury
NMSA Publications Editor

v

Preface

The Team Process in the Middle School: A Handbook for Teachers was initially created as a guide for classroom teachers who desire to work in clusters or teams to address the unique learning needs of middle school students. Successful teaming at the middle school level depends upon the leadership skills of the building principal as well as the motivation, skills, and abilities of teachers to work together to deliver an instructional program that responds to the physical, intellectual, social-emotional, and moral developmental needs of early adolescents. This third and expanded edition has the same goals.

Most middle school teachers have not taken specific courses in the team process. Yet, it is imperative that middle school teachers function effectively in teams if the middle school concept is to be successful in this nation and around the world. Therefore, staff development programs must help teachers learn about the team process until such time as undergraduate and/or graduate courses address this topic adequately.

This publication is largely a description of the efforts of teachers working in Baltimore County, Maryland. These procedures can be replicated in any middle level school or district. Baltimore County middle school teachers understand the real potential of the middle school concept and recognize that the team process is a vital element in achieving that goal.

I would like to thank two people for their help in producing the third edition of this monograph:

— My wife, Ilene, for typing and re-typing the manuscript.

— My friend, John H. Lounsbury, for his continuing and untiring efforts on behalf of the middle school movement in general and in particular for his help in editing and managing the production of *The Team Process: A Handbook for Teachers.*

Elliot Y. Merenbloom

1

Characteristics of an Effective Middle School

Successful team process experiences in the middle school should be based upon a thorough understanding of the characteristics of an effective middle school as well as the middle school concept itself. Although the movement started in the early 1960s, the literature continues to define more fully the meaning of the middle school concept. All that happens in a middle level school should be based upon the foundations described in the first three chapters. Working in groups or on an independent basis, teachers should keep in mind the twelve characteristics of an effective middle school that are presented below. In many ways, the team process becomes the way to achieve the elements of the middle school concept.

AN EFFECTIVE MIDDLE SCHOOL:

1. **Features a program that responds to the physical, intellectual, social-emotional, and moral needs of early adolescents.**

Current data about the physical, intellectual, social-emotional, and moral development of the early adolescent must be examined. Terms such as *earlier onset of puberty*, *unevenness of growth*, *cognitive development*, *peer group*, *self-concept*, *sensitivity*, and *values education* need to be internalized. Then, educators should identify the implications of each of these data elements to realize the importance of team process, counseling and guidance, variety of activities needed within a lesson, concrete examples as concepts are introduced, skill development, peer tutors, home base program, and consistent discipline policies. Finally, educators should identify and integrate implications of the data from all of these categories to analyze the curriculum, school organization options, nature of the learning environment, reading program, and role of the classroom teacher. Specific aspects of the program must be based on identified needs of the student population.

2. Has a set of documents to guide all aspects of the program.

A number of key documents are needed to guide the development of the middle school program. There needs to be a clear definition of what a middle school is or ought to be. Once this definition is developed by the school district and/or the local school, it should be shared with the community.

A second critical document is a needs assessment which identifies the physical, intellectual, social-emotional, and moral needs of the students assigned to the school and places these needs in the context of the current school program. Pupil data to be included in a needs assessment are standardized test scores, achievement records, family history, interests, goals, and learning styles.

Thirdly, a philosophy and set of goals should be developed to reflect the overall direction of the school's program. Via a broad statement of philosophy and rather specific set of goals and objectives, the faculty and community can agree on their expectations of the program. This information may also be referred to as the mission statement of the school.

Finally, a rationale should be developed to give the underlying reasons for the major facets of the program. A rationale might include sub-headings as: interdisciplinary teams, grouping, curriculum, intramural program, and the home base/advisory program.

3. Possesses a definite curriculum plan that includes organized knowledge, skills, and personal development activities.

Alexander (1969) recommended a curriculum model that consists of factual information, skill development, and activities designed to help pupils understand and cope with the changes which they are or will be experiencing. Each course within the curriculum should feature these three elements. As teachers work together in the team planning process, efforts should be made to correlate content, skills, and personal development activities. Thus, this curriculum model becomes the basis of the team approach to instruction. The place of a home base/advisory program in the curriculum must be addressed.

4. Has a clearly established program of studies based upon the concept of exploration and provides opportunities for student growth.

The program of studies should clearly reflect the needs of early adolescents. Courses that comprise the program for each grade level should reflect unique needs of students of that age. Certain subjects such as language arts and mathematics should be offered every year. Within the specific units of study for the course, evidence of growth and maturation should exist. Students need an opportunity to explore a great variety of areas such as music, technology, or art rather than specializing via an elective program. Exploration should occur within each subject as well. In addition to the curricular experiences, pupils benefit greatly from an extensive co-curricular/activities/intramural program. Social-emotional needs of the early adolescent can be met via these aspects of the program. The goal is to develop a well-rounded young adult; this can be accomplished without an extensive electives program at this level.

5. **Builds on the successes of elementary education and prepares students for success in high school.**

An effective middle school is a transitional experience for pupils who are at various stages of approaching adolescence. The program should build on the successes of elementary education by focusing on the learning needs of each student as an individual, having a sequential approach to skill development, providing for the correlation of content, and having a team approach to teaching. The teaching of reading and related communication skills should be emphasized in every subject area every period of the day. In turn, the middle school experience should adequately prepare students for the ninth grade program in high school where students will likely have various teachers in a more departmentalized approach and have more decisions to make with regard to the curriculum as well as the extra-curricular program. The middle school should serve as a meaningful connection between elementary and high school education. Articulation activities are needed to ensure the greatest possible continuity between elementary and middle schools as well as middle schools and high schools. Articulation activities must include the active involvement of teachers and focus on the total scope and sequence of the Pre K-12 curriculum. Pupils must be oriented as they move from the elementary school to the middle school as well as from the middle school to the high school. Furthermore, students should be oriented to their unique opportunities at each grade level of the middle school experience.

6. **Employs teachers who focus on learning needs of pupils, use varied teaching techniques, and actively involve students.**

Each middle school teacher should know the special learning needs of each pupil. Early adolescent students have diverse learning needs that are the result of individualized timetables for physical, intellectual, social-emotional, and moral development. Appropriate techniques include student-to-student interaction; clear, concise structure for activities; adequate motivation, readiness, and goal-setting for each activity; clear transitions to connect the various activities; the inductive process; lessons that move from the concrete to the abstract; and enrichment activities for formal thinkers.

7. **Organizes teaching teams using block-of-time and modular scheduling.**

Teaching teams provide an excellent opportunity to strengthen the instructional program, focus on the learning needs of pupils, and facilitate flexibility. Interdisciplinary teams usually consist of two to five teachers of four or five subjects who plan for and teach two or more classes during the same periods of the day. In grade six, two teachers could coordinate an interdisciplinary approach to the curriculum for a common group of students. A disciplinary team involves two or more teachers of the same subject who teach two or more classes of that subject at the same time. Block-of-time scheduling permits the teachers who teach at the same time to also be available for a common planning period.

Modular scheduling strategies permit teachers to subdivide the total block-of-time for teaching into various modules or time periods to accommodate all aspects of the instructional program. Teachers use a variety of team building activities to create a cohesive and unique identity for that team. The role and function of a team must be clearly delineated. Via inservice training, teachers may learn a number of team planning techniques to enhance the learning process for students.

8. **Emphasizes the guidance and counseling function of staff members by providing for a home base program, stressing the importance of self-concept, and providing a positive climate.**

Every teacher in the building is, to a degree, a counselor by being sensitive to the needs of students. A student should be able to turn to any member of the professional staff with whom the student feels comfortable to seek help with a problem. Traditionally, secondary school teachers are responsible only for addressing cognitive or informational needs of students. Middle school teachers, however, are asked to attend to affective or emotional needs of a student's development as well.

Home base or teacher advisory programs may include orientation to the new school and/or grade, techniques to resolve conflict, study skills, and communication skills. All aspects of the instructional program should focus on self-concept. The overall climate of the school should be positive so that youngsters will grow and learn in a healthy environment. A leadership team approach may be utilized to increase the sense of belonging on the part of the faculty.

9. **Promotes flexibility in implementing the schedule to meet varying needs of students.**

Flexibility is a key word in the middle school concept. Since students are in a highly individualized stage of development, the schedule and program must be flexible in order to respond to changes and needs evident in various stages of transition. The master schedule should provide broad, general parameters but can and should be altered by the teaching teams on a daily, weekly, or monthly basis. Every class meeting need not be for fifty minutes. In some cases, classes can be less than fifty minutes; and, for specific purposes, classes could be extended to sixty or seventy minutes. On a weekly basis, special modules could be arranged for spelling, handwriting, or a skills lab program. Pupils could be grouped and regrouped as needed. Teaching sections within a team could rotate schedules, special arrangements could be made for field trips, or an entire team's schedule could be exchanged with another team's schedule on a semester or trimester basis.

10. Actively involves parents in various aspects of the school experience.

As in the elementary school, parents may play a key role in the learning experiences of middle school students. Schools must exert even greater efforts to make parents active participants, not just passive observers. Parents must learn about middle school curriculum and about the uniqueness of early adolescents. Parents may be called upon to volunteer their skills and expertise. Appropriate systems must be developed to help parents monitor the progress of their child in keeping with the need to provide children with greater opportunities for independence. Parents must be able to make adjustments called for by developmental tasks of early adolescence. The issues of dependence/independence, group identity, peer group pressures, and search for sophistication require appropriate strategies for parents during these critical years of adjustment. Middle schools must make parents feel welcome and help parents realize that they are partners in the learning process.

11. Evaluates the program on a regular basis and makes changes that enhance learning.

Evaluation takes place in many ways. Surveys, questionnaires, feedback from parents, reports from regional accrediting groups, classroom observations, and evaluations of individual teachers provide important information which indicates if a program is succeeding. Those responsible for schools must monitor the extent to which learning is actually occurring and act accordingly. Goal-setting may emerge from the evaluative process and facilitate the improvement of the school's program. It is not necessary to wait until the end of the school year to make changes. Incremental transition is encouraged to facilitate a gradual implementation of the middle school concept and to dispel any notion that all aspects of the middle school program must be implemented at the same time.

12. Features a staff development program that enables the faculty to successfully implement the elements of an effective middle school.

Staff development is an essential factor in the successful transition to the middle school concept. Based upon the change process, a variety of staff development approaches should be used to obtain faculty involvement. As faculty and staff become involved, successful implementation follows.

An effective staff development program includes definite goals, objectives, and an organizational plan; sufficient lead time prior to the implementation of the project; a sustained, sequential, continuous effort; sensitivity to the needs of teachers; active involvement of the participants; and provision to train teachers newly assigned to the school. Staff development is most effective when it is a shared responsibility between the school district and the individual school and, within the individual school, between the faculty and the administration.

A process/content approach is suggested. Process refers to techniques, procedures, or strategies to achieve a goal; process implies methodology such as inservice courses, summer workshops, or visits to other middle schools. Content includes the study of early adolescent behavior, appropriate teaching strategies, and organizational options. It is the interaction of process and content that facilitates adult learning.

SUMMARY

These twelve characteristics describe an effective middle school. The "bottom line" is to create an effective climate for learning for pupils in the middle grades. As an activity, an entire faculty or a team of teachers should answer the questions contained in the activity.

Activity:

1. How many of these twelve characteristics are evident in our school or on our team?

2. Which characteristic(s) should be a high priority for implementation or reinforcement?

3. What will our strategy be to implement or reinforce the characteristic(s)?

4. How will we evaluate our efforts to implement or reinforce the characteristic(s)?

5. How will we select the next priority for implementation or reinforcement?

2

Responding To The Needs
Of Early Adolescent Learners

As teachers prepare to work in a middle school setting, they should become very familiar with three major elements of the middle school concept: (1) the needs of early adolescent students, (2) a curriculum model for the middle level, and (3) a variety of options for organizing middle level schools for effective instruction. This chapter will focus on the needs of students; the next chapter will highlight thoughts about curriculum and how to deliver that curriculum.

In this chapter, teachers will have an opportunity to learn about the physical, intellectual, social-emotional, and moral needs of the early adolescent and then to identify the implications of the content in each of the four areas. Finally, teachers will be able to review data in all categories to list overall implications for curriculum, organization of the school, nature of the learning environment, role of the teacher, and the reading program in the middle school.

In such a simulation, middle school teachers will have the opportunity to recreate the birth process of the middle school movement. The founders of the middle school movement examined data in these categories and proceeded to create a program that was responsive to the unique needs of the early adolescent. Perhaps the real beauty of the middle school concept is that a group of teachers, administrators, guidance counselors, and central office personnel can design a middle school in the same fashion that the original middle schools were created in the early 1960s.

PHYSICAL DEVELOPMENT

Early adolescence is a period of extensive physical growth. There appears to be one blueprint for the growth of girls and a separate plan for boys. Girls may begin to enter puberty as early as 8 1/2 years of age and are finished by the tenth grade in most cases. Boys, on the other hand, tend to lag two years behind girls. The average age for the appearance of pubic hair in boys is 12 1/2; the average age for the beginning of boys' most rapid growth in height is 14 years. Males may not complete puberty until age 20.

Two major conclusions can be derived from this information: (1) there are both early and late maturers among both girls and boys and (2) students in grades 5-8 demonstrate the greatest variation in physical growth of any clustering of grade levels. The key words are *individual differences* and *variations* in growth patterns. The basis for the concept of flexibility results from information about the physical development of early adolescents.

A significant study of the physical development of the transescent was the Boyce Medical Study, conducted by Dr. Allen Drash and Dr. Donald Eichhorn (1975). This study looked at the impact of biological maturation on the learning process and found a high correlation between learning and maturation. As a result, the authors of the study recommended a non-graded or developmental age concept based on Tanner's stages of adolescence: pre-pubescent, emerging adolescence, and adolescence. Continuous progress teaching/learning strategies were suggested.

A major outcome of this research on physical development was the recognition of a need for home base or advisor/advisee programs that would enable transescents to better understand and cope with the changes taking place. Because they are concerned with bodily changes that accompany sexual maturation, health and sex education must be key elements in the curriculum. As teachers plan for lessons, they should recognize the short attention span, restlessness, and fatigue of these students. Physical education should be scheduled on a daily basis, as middle school students need this physical activity because of increased energy. Physical education teachers should be aware that bodily changes cause awkward, uncoordinated behavior. Finally, adults must be sensitive to the feelings of students at various stages of development and careful not to reinforce feelings of inadequacy.

INTELLECTUAL DEVELOPMENT

There is also a wide range of mental development occurring between the ages of 10 and 14. Piaget described a period of concrete operations between the ages of 7 and 11 that was followed by a period of formal operations beginning at approximately age 11 and continuing to age 15. During this latter period, the student begins to hypothesize, utilize logic and reasoning in decision making, yet still have some difficulty with concepts such as government, race, or religion as abstract thoughts. Middle school teachers have realized that not all students move from Piaget's concrete stage to formal thinking at ages 11 or 12 and that concrete examples are essential to the learning process.

The studies of Epstein and Toepfer (1978) in the area of brain growth periodization seem to have substantiated Piaget's thinking from a biological point of view and also have provided further insight into the adolescent's intellectual processes. Growth spurts occur between ages 2-4, 6-8, 10-12, and 14-16 as a result of cell expansion. Growth occurs at some time during these periods, not necessarily on a given month or day. Between ages 10-12, the average growth in mental age is 38-40 months. Plateaus occur at ages 4-6, 8-10, and 12-14. Between ages 12-14, for example, the average growth in mental age is 7 months.

Probably the best known application of the work of Piaget and Epstein is the Cognitive Levels Matching Project at the Shoreham-Wading River Middle School. In *Cognitive Matched Instruction in Action,* Esther Fusco and her associates (1987) describe efforts of teachers to become sensitive to child development. Teachers assessed the developmental levels of students and also evaluated the requirements implicit in curricular tasks. As a result, teachers became adept in adjusting the appropriateness of curriculum to the developmental stages of students; and, learning was enhanced.

During these plateau periods, it is felt that students can learn but cannot initiate higher order thinking skills than demonstrated at the growth stage. Teachers, therefore, should utilize skills and levels already achieved, teach skills and processes in addition to content, drop back to the concrete when abstract ideas are not understood, teach new facts and new information within thinking skills initiated by the end of the 10-12 growth period, devote class time to skill development and self-concept, and provide teaching strategies that actively involve students in the learning process.

SOCIAL-EMOTIONAL DEVELOPMENT

Middle level educators must recognize the social-emotional developmental problems of the early adolescent. Often these occur as the body matures and the youngster becomes very sensitive about the changes that have or have not taken place.

The transescent needs help and support in controlling emotions. Achievement in school may be blocked by emotional disorganization. Major topics in this area of include:

Group membership. The early adolescent has a strong need to belong to a group. The need and search for peer approval increases as the importance of adult approval decreases. Students will experiment with new slang and behavior as they search for a social position within their group. Participation in a group is important and can be a positive or negative influence. Through classroom situations, middle school teachers can offer students positive growth opportunities in various aspects of group membership. In many cases, middle school students will turn to the group to cover up for feelings of inadequacy.

Self-concept. Earlier perceptions of self are frequently altered by changes that occur at puberty. It is important for educators to realize that this understanding of self is based on an internal frame of reference and may not be accurate. Early adolescents tend to be self-conscious and are sensitive to personal criticism. They believe that their problems, feelings, and experiences are unique to themselves. Self-concept is frequently affected by unkind statements from adults as well as peers.

Need for catharsis. Middle school students benefit from an opportunity to openly share their thoughts or emotions with an adult or another student who has been trained as a listener. Middle school students have widely varying moods with peaks of intensity and unpredictability. They react overtly to ridicule, embarrassment, and rejection. To achieve this catharsis, the individual must have a feeling of acceptance, and the communication should be encouraged by reflection and other non-directive methods.

Ethnic identification process. Dr. Geneva Gay (1978) suggests that the presence of ethnicity during early adolescence further complicates social-emotional development. For culturally different students, identity dilemmas result from new demands associated with racial backgrounds. To help minority students, the school curriculum should include structured experiences in social growth and development.

Sex role identification. Sexual awareness increases as secondary sex characteristics begin to appear. The early adolescent exhibits intense concern about physical growth and maturity as profound changes occur. They must find out what it means to be male or female. Although this process begins early in life, it is affected by changes that occur at puberty. Middle school students behave in ways associated with their sex as sex role identification strengthens. They frequently wonder if they are normal and if others will like and accept them.

Peer approval. The peer group comprises the primary social world of early adolescents; thus, feedback from the peer group is very important. Because peer groups offer security and early adolescents want recognition for their efforts, pressure exists to conform to group norms.

Independence from adults. A major developmental task for this age is the search for autonomy. Although early adolescents yearn to be independent, they are still dependent upon adults for both identity and acceptance. Middle school students model behavior after older, esteemed students as well as non-parent adults. Even though they are dependent on parental beliefs and values, they do everything possible to be seen as individuals. Many conflicts arise because parents do not want to grant independence. The road to independence is paved with ambivalence, inconsistency, and conflict for the early adolescent.

Search for sophistication. Middle school students exhibit immature behavior because their social skills frequently lag behind intellectual and physical maturity. They experiment with new slang words and behavior as they try to be sophisticated. They like fads, especially those shunned by adults and highlighted by the media. Unfortunately, the media encourages sophistication at an earlier chronological age. Search for sophistication is closely related to self-concept and the perceived need for independence. Adults must realize that this search involves much experimentation, but they can provide information and counseling as viable alternatives to certain behaviors and actions.

MORAL DEVELOPMENT

Adults want their children to have instruction in moral behavior, although some may disagree over what is taught or how it is taught. School systems across the nation are becoming more and more involved in moral development or values education programs.

The work of the late Dr. Lawrence Kohlberg (1973) of Harvard serves as the foundation for many of these programs. Kohlberg, using the term *moral reasoning*, suggested that teachers use moral dilemmas with their students. Kohlberg's work is considered cognitive moral development. The term *cognitive* stresses organized thought processes, the term *moral* involves decision-making in situations where unusual values come in conflict, and *development* suggests that patterns of thinking about moral issues improve qualitatively over time. Research in this area is still in the beginning stages. Unfortunately, the link between reasoning morally and acting morally is weak.

Baltimore County, Maryland Public Schools (1983) embarked upon a program of values education based on the theme "1984 and Beyond: A Reaffirmation of Values." As a part of this project, the school system identified ten premises regarding values education.

1. Values education needs to be defined.

2. There should be recognition that a common core of values exists within our pluralistic society.

3. There should be an awareness of the existence of conflicts among acceptable values.

4. There should be a greater awareness by teachers and administrators of the potential role of values in education and of their part in transmitting values.

5. Educators should be aware that values are taught implicitly and explicitly through the curriculum and by practices throughout the school system.

6. Educators should be aware of the values and ethics perspectives of the community as expressed by representatives of the public and private sectors.

7. Educators should understand that society supports an increasingly important role for the public schools in values education.

8. Knowledge gained from research in the field of values education and the developmental stages of children and youth should be applied to our approach to the topic.

9. Goals for the outcome of values education in terms of student behavior and character development should be established.

10. A recognized philosophy of values education and commitment to its implementation should be adopted by the school system and communicated to all related groups.

It is possible, according to the Baltimore County model, to identify a series of values to be incorporated into an educational program. The following values comprise a common core of values for a school or school district:

Compassion	Objectivity
Courtesy	Order
Critical Inquiry	Patriotism
Due Process	Rational Consent
Equality of Opportunity	Reasoned Argument
Freedom of Thought and Action	Respect for Others' Rights
Honesty	Responsibility
Human Worth and Dignity	Responsible Citizenship
Integrity	Rule of Law
Justice	Self-respect
Loyalty	Tolerance
Knowledge	Truth

The middle school organizational plan offers a unique approach for teaching moral development, values education topics, or a common core of values. Most topics can be taught through the various subject areas in the context of existing curriculum. Additionally, certain topics can be approached through home base or teacher/advisory programs. Ideally, the interaction of teaching in content areas and the discussions in the home base area reinforce one another. As students recognize that these values have importance throughout the school, they will integrate or assimilate them more readily.

SUMMARY

The middle school movement is a response to the needs of the early adolescent student. Teachers must become familiar with data about the physical, intellectual, social-emotional, and moral developmental needs of these students and then identify implications of those data to create a model middle school program. The following activity provides the structure necessary for teachers, administrators, and counselors to have that experience.

Activity:

Using information in this chapter as well as other resources on the physical, intellectual, social-emotional, and moral development of the early adolescent, teachers should complete the following chart. After summarizing characteristics for each area, implications of each area should be identified. Finally, the overall implications should be developed using the implications from each of the four areas. Teachers should work in multidisciplinary groups on the activity.

RESPONDING TO THE NEEDS OF THE EARLY ADOLESCENT LEARNER

I. CHARACTERISTICS

A. Physical
  1.
  2.
  3.
  4.
  5.
  6.
  7.
  8.

B. Intellectual
  1.
  2.
  3.
  4.
  5.
  6.
  7.
  8.

C. Social-Emotional
  1.
  2.
  3.
  4.
  5.
  6.
  7.
  8.

D. Moral
  1.
  2.
  3.
  4.
  5.
  6.
  7.
  8.

II. IMPLICATIONS OF EACH AREA

A. Physical
  1.Students need a variety of activities because of their short attention span.
  2.Physical education classes must be adjusted for the varying needs of pupils.
  3.
  4.
  5.

B. Intellectual
  1. Teachers should use concrete examples in concept development.
  2. Pupils should have opportunities for independent study in each subject.
  3.
  4.
  5.

C. Social-Emotional
  1.Teachers should receive assistance in developing counseling and communication skills.
  2. The exploratory program should be a vital part of the curriculum.
  3.
  4.
  5.

D. **Moral**
   1. Teachers need to be consistent in their expectations of student behavior.
   2. Literature and social studies programs provide excellent opportunities for teaching moral dilemmas.
   3.
   4.
   5.

III. OVERALL IMPLICATIONS OF ALL AREAS

A. **Curriculum**
   1.
   2.
   3.
   4.
   5.

B. **Organization of the School**
   1.
   2.
   3.
   4.
   5.

C. **Nature of the Learning Environment**
   1.
   2.
   3.
   4.
   5.

D. **Role of the Teacher**
   1.
   2.
   3.
   4.
   5.

E. **Reading Program**
   1.
   2.
   3.
   4.
   5.

3

Delivering the
Curriculum to Students

In addition to learning how to respond to the needs of the early adolescent learner, middle school teachers should understand the basic fundamentals of curriculum theory for the middle level and then recognize the variety of options for delivering that curriculum to students in grades 6, 7, and 8. This chapter will help teachers recognize that middle school curriculum is a response to the needs of students and that options can be studied to identify the organizational plan that is most appropriate for the learning needs of students in a given school district or school.

A MODEL FOR CURRICULUM

William Alexander (1969) suggests a model for middle school curriculum that consists of three major components — organized knowledge, skills, and personal development.

1. Organized knowledge refers to factual information contained in the subject matter of all courses in the curriculum - English, social studies, mathematics, science, French, Spanish, art, music, home economics, physical education, technology education, or any other course in the directory. Middle school curriculum must have a clear focus on factual information because early adolescent students are ready for this emphasis. Middle level students must also learn how to secure factual information in future settings, in the classroom, or on an independent basis.

2. Middle school teachers have a major responsibility for teaching skills. In elementary schools, the teaching of skills is the major focus. Middle school students need this emphasis on skills as well. The teaching of reading must include emphasis on vocabulary development, comprehension, study skills, and functional reading. Additionally, students must be competent in writing, computing, listening, and reference skills.

3. Personal development refers to information and activities needed by the early adolescent learner to better understand growth and development. It is felt that the more the early adolescent understands the changes about to occur, the better that student will be in coping with or adjusting to those changes. Each subject area should have topics or units that address the personal development issue. For example, a language arts unit entitled "The Outsider" or a unit in French entitled "Going To School In France" would help the student learn about developmental problems. Additionally, all of the teachers of the interdisciplinary team or all teachers of the school could work together to present the home base or teacher/advisory program which is also an aspect of the personal development phase of curriculum.

There are two applications of Alexander's model. First, the curriculum for each subject area should include experiences in the categories of organized knowledge, skills, and personal development. The content of every course should be subdivided into these three categories. To practice this application, teachers should work by areas to complete the chart below. Only major topics or skills should be listed for each subject at each grade level.

Grade_____   **Subject**_____

Organized Knowledge
   1.
   2.
   3.
   4.
   5.
   6.
   7.
   8.
   9.
  10.

Skills
   1.
   2.
   3.
   4.
   5.
   6.
   7.
   8.
   9.
  10.

Personal Development
   1.
   2.
   3.
   4.

     5.
     6.
     7.
     8.
     9.
     10.

The second application involves the function of interdisciplinary teams. A team of teachers should make every effort to correlate organized knowledge, skills, and personal development topics. Interdisciplinary connections help pupils see the unity or relationships among the topics, units, or subjects being studied. Correlation can and should occur as teachers deliver content, skills, and the home base or teacher/advisory program. Ideally, curriculum guides should be written on an interdisciplinary basis. If not, teachers should review summaries of their subject areas to create a composite picture of connections possible. The following chart is an example of how the content in several units in English 7 can be correlated with topics in social studies, science, and mathematics at the same grade level.

ENGLISH GRADE 7

ENGLISH	SOCIAL STUDIES	SCIENCE	MATHEMATICS
Stereotypes in Fact and Fiction	Africa	Scientists; Experimenting	Decimals; Graphs
Designs in Art and Poetry	Africa		Geometry
Knights and Champions	Europe	Building Models	Gathering Data; Measurement
Conflict: The Heart of the Matter	Africa; Middle East	Analyzing Data	Probability
Communication	Africa; Middle East; Russia	Experimenting	Math Symbols; Word Problems

Students benefit when teams of teachers work cooperatively to teach and reinforce skills. A skill-of-the-week program enables all teachers of the team to coordinate their efforts to introduce, reinforce, and evaluate a skill taught in the context of each subject area. *Reading and Writing in the Middle School,* a guide to teaching skills for middle level teachers in Baltimore County, Maryland (1985), suggests a number of topics that could be presented over the course of the year as teachers work together.

     1. Notebook Organization Checklist
     2. Manuscript Form
     3. Assignment Sheet
     4. Home Study Skills
     5. Vocabulary Page

6. Anatomy of a Textbook
7. Reference Materials
8. Methods of Reading
9. Preparing an Oral Report
10. Taking Notes from a Written Source
11. Taking Notes from an Oral Source
12. Conducting Research
13. Bibliographic Format
14. Having a Writing Conference with Yourself: Narration
15. Having a Writing Conference with Yourself: Exposition
16. Punctuation Review
17. Spelling Aids
18. Capitalization Review
19. Independent Reading
20. Test Taking
21. Solving a Problem with Numbers
22. Solving Other Types of Problems

Finally, teachers are encouraged to work together to deliver the home base program. These topics are typically included:

Decision Making: Throughout the middle school years, students must make choices about their educational future as well as their personal lives. Students are introduced to the steps in decision-making which include identifying the problem, generating alternatives, evaluating each alternative, choosing the best alternative, and creating a plan of action.

Resolving Conflicts: Middle school students often find themselves involved in conflicts with others. This unit has been created to help them deal with their feelings in working through these problems. Problems with "being bullied," feeling "put down," making friends, determining values, and identifying potential irritating situations can be included.

Careers: Grades 6, 7, and 8 are an appropriate time to begin the process of investigating the world of work. This unit contains materials for teaching about career clusters and matching skills with occupations.

Understanding Myself and Others: The concept of self is redefined and shaped during the middle years. A unit on self-esteem and self-concept enables an early adolescent to explore feelings about self-worth and evaluate feedback from others.

Communication Skills: Early adolescents experience difficulty with interpersonal relationships. Information about verbal and non-verbal communication, openness and trust, and problem solving skills help the student improve in this area.

High School Orientation: Middle school personnel have a responsibility to help eighth grade students prepare for the high school experience. Registration, including the introduction to the requirements for high school graduation, and adjustment to life on the high school campus are topics to be covered.

Other home base units are:

1. Study Skills
2. Drug and Alcohol Resistance Education (D.A.R.E.)
3. Growing Up in Various Cultures
4. I Am Lovable and Capable (I.A.L.A.C.)
5. Understanding Similarities and Differences
6. Helping the Handicapped
7. Interpersonal Relationships
8. Compassion
9. Courtesy
10. Honesty
11. Human Worth and Dignity
12. Integrity
13. Justice
14. Loyalty
15. Respect for the Rights of Others
16. Self-Management: Rights and Responsibilities
17. Self-Management: Planning
18. Team Building
19. Community Service

To help an interdisciplinary group of teachers identify correlations on a regular, systematic basis, the following model is suggested.

A MODEL FOR CURRICULUM WORKSHEET

ORGANIZED KNOWLEDGE TOPIC_____

English:
Mathematics:
Social Studies:
Science:
Art:
Music:
Physical Education:
Home Economics:
Technology Education:

SKILL TOPIC_____

English:
Mathematics:
Social Studies:
Science:
Art:
Music:
Physical Education:
Home Economics:
Technology Education:

PERSONAL DEVELOPMENT TOPIC_____

English:
Mathematics:
Social Studies:
Science:
Art:
Music:
Physical Education:
Home Economics:
Technology Education:

Teachers need to work as a team in order to provide a balanced curriculum that responds to pupils' needs. This approach should insure that the curriculum is responsive to the needs of students.

ORGANIZATIONAL OPTIONS

One of the best ways a middle school can be responsive to the needs of the early adolescent is to utilize some form of team planning/teaching. Some of the specific reasons for team teaching at this level include an opportunity to (1) help pupils make the transition from a self-contained elementary classroom to the departmentalization of the secondary grades, (2) help students see the wholeness that exists in learning, both in content and skills, (3) emphasize the child as well as subject matter, (4) provide consistency to an age group that desperately needs structure and consistency, (5) create a family-like atmosphere in an age when fewer and fewer students know the real meaning of the word *family*, (6) facilitate various grouping arrangements for students, (7) enable teachers to subdivide blocks-of-time to best meet the unique needs of students, (8) provide for increased professional growth of teachers through cooperative planning, sharing of materials, and cooperative teaching, (9) provide more opportunities for resource personnel to be directly involved in the instructional program, and (10) provide for the unique guidance needs of early adolescent students.

Simply stated, team teaching involves a group of teachers providing instruction to a group of students. In some cases, teachers may plan together during common team planning periods but then return to their individual classrooms and work independently with their own classes. In other cases, it may involve teachers in cooperative planning and then actually teaching together. Several classes may be brought together for large group instruction or for an organized, independent study program. The identity of each of the classes may be lost as the total instructional program unfolds. Another example of team teaching could feature small group instruction. In this case, students may be regrouped according to interests or ability levels regardless of the teaching section to which they were initially assigned. Finally, team teaching could include a group of teachers working together to correlate content and skill development on a regular, systematic basis or to present a thematic unit as they teach different subjects to a common group of students.

There are three types of team teaching. An interdisciplinary team involves two or more teachers working together to coordinate instruction in three, four, or five subject areas. For example, an English, social studies, mathematics, and science teacher could work together with four teaching sections to create an interdisciplinary approach to learning the content of those four areas.

Benefits of the interdisciplinary team approach include:

1. Students have subject matter specialists for each subject, but there is coordination of the total instructional program.

2. Beyond the standard curriculum guides, thematic interdisciplinary units as well as specific interdisciplinary activities can be planned to meet the needs of pupils.

3. Teachers can work as a team to focus on the needs of pupils.

4. Content, skills, and personnel development activities can be correlated.

5. Planning periods can be used for pupil and parent conferences.

6. A discipline code for the entire team can be consistently implemented.

7. The use of contiguous classrooms permits students to change classes at times decided by a team of teachers without disturbing other classes.

8. Block-of-time and flexible scheduling can facilitate fundamental aspects of the program.

9. Teaching sections can be organized on a homogeneous, heterogeneous, or contiguous basis; regrouping is possible.

There are some other factors to consider in implementing the interdisciplinary approach.

1. The time needed for team planning must come from the teachers' regular work day. In districts that insure teachers one duty free period per day, the team planning period becomes another situation where teachers are not in direct contact with students.

2. Staffing guidelines may not be adequate for reasonable class size. As teachers are given a duty free period as well as a team planning period each day, average class size figures may increase.

3. The block-of-time (20-25 periods per week) is a high scheduling priority.

4. Teachers not included in the interdisciplinary team structure may be excluded from the planning process.

5. The responsibility of classroom teachers is expanded. Many teachers may not feel adequately prepared for this type of assignment. The teaching contract may set a limit on the number of teacher preparations per day.

6. The personalities of the teachers involved must be compatible.

A disciplinary team involves two or more teachers of the same subject who work together to present that course to two or more sections scheduled at the same time each day. The major thrust, obviously, is to find the best way of teaching that course to meet the learning needs of the students assigned to those sections. As an example, two Algebra I teachers could combine their efforts in teaching 50 students. Over the course of the year, the 50 students could be re-grouped between these two teachers according to the students' strengths and weaknesses.

Special features of the disciplinary team are:

1. Two or more teachers plan instruction in one subject area for a group of pupils who can then be grouped or regrouped for varying purposes in that subject.

2. Team meets on a regular basis for planning and evaluating the program.

3. Program in that subject is tailored to the needs of pupils.

4. Teachers have an opportunity to specialize within that subject area.

5. Special programs can be developed for the special needs of pupils in a particular subject area.

6. A team of subject matter specialists provides instruction in one curricular area.

7. Department head can coordinate efforts of all teams in that department.

8. Teachers can teach more than one grade level.

9. Excellent opportunities exist for curriculum development and implementation at the local school level.

10. Student has more than one teacher for a particular content area.

11. Experienced teachers help novices.

12. Enrichment and remediation can be offered in both large and small group settings.

Potential limitations of single subject teams include:

1. Pupil needs to adjust to as many as six or seven different teams of pupils and teachers.

2. Less focus on personal development and less integration of skills may occur; student sees skills in isolation.

3. Teachers must agree on content of instructional program as well as methodology.

4. Pupil does not see correlation of various content areas.

5. Focus on student may be sacrificed for specialization in content areas.

6. More hall traffic is generated.

A third approach to team teaching is frequently called the core/combination subject team. A mini-version of the interdisciplinary team, this model involves two or three teachers of two or three subjects. Examples of core/combination subject teams are English/social studies/art or English/social studies or art/music. In these situations, the two or three teachers have the opportunity to better coordinate their efforts in delivering the instructional program. Core/combination subject teaming affords more opportunities for large and small group instruction, regrouping within and between subjects, correlation, and the opportunity for a student to spend more time in one of these subject areas.

The three types of team organization are not mutually exclusive. An overall plan for instruction in a given middle school could involve all three options. In addition to selecting when to use each of the options, consideration should be given to the number of teachers on a teaching team.

Self-contained classes — One teacher could be responsible for all subjects. In the sixth grade, for example, one teacher could teach English, social studies, reading, mathematics, and science to a class of 26 students. This organizational plan is similar to the elementary school approach. The students would leave that teacher's classroom for art, music, and physical education. This approach is effective in working with students who are having difficulty adjusting to middle school. As an alternative program, pupils could be transferred from the self-contained classes to a two, three, or four member team according to the progress of that student.

Two teacher team — In this option, two teachers are scheduled on a paralleled basis with two groups or classes. These two teachers are responsible for the reading/language arts, science, mathematics, and social studies programs for a block of 25 periods per week. Both teachers could teach reading/language arts at the same time, thus re-regrouping students according to reading levels. One of the teachers could then teach science to both sections; the other teacher could teach social studies to both sections. These two subjects could be grouped on a heterogeneous or homogeneous basis. Finally, the students could be re-grouped for mathematics according to achievement levels in that subject. Both teachers would be teaching mathematics at the same time. In the seventh grade, one teacher could teach English and social studies while the other teacher is responsible for mathematics and science. When reading is a part of the curriculum, teachers could share responsibility for that course.

Three teacher team — Three teachers could be scheduled at the same time for three classes. All three teachers could teach reading/language arts at the same time; students would be assigned to teachers according to their achievement levels so that homogeneous grouping is in effect. After this two hour block for reading/language arts, students could then go to each of the three teachers for science, mathematics, and social studies. One of the three teachers becomes the specialist for each content area. Groupings could be homogeneous or heterogeneous. Teachers have an opportunity to specialize but still work together in planning the reading/language arts program.

Four teacher team — Using a more traditional secondary model, four sections can work together with four teachers for five content areas. One teacher specializes in language arts; one, social studies; one, mathematics; and one, science. For one given period of the day, all four teachers teach reading, permitting the students to be grouped homogeneously for reading but homogeneously or heterogeneously for the other four subjects.

Five teacher team — Probably at the eighth grade level, this model would enable students to have five different teachers for five different subjects as part of the preparation for high school. The five subjects would typically be English, social studies, mathematics, science, and French or Spanish. Reading could also be the fifth subject on that team.

SUMMARY

Middle school is both a curricular and organizational issue. Alexander's curriculum model is a response to the learning needs of the early adolescent pupil and provides excellent structure for how teaching teams can function. Each individual school or school district should carefully study the pro's and con's of the interdisciplinary, disciplinary, and core/combination subject team models. Next, consideration should be given to the number of teachers on a team. What should result is a pattern (p. 27) for team organization that reflects that school's or district's approach to delivering instruction according to the unique needs of middle level students.

Activity:

Teachers and administrative/supervisory personnel should answer these questions and then prepare a pattern of school organization. One pattern is included as a sample only.

1. For our school or school system, what are the advantages and limitations of each type of team?

2. For our school or school system, what are the advantages and limitations of a two teacher, three teacher, four teacher, or five teacher team?

3. What is the faculty's preference for an overall plan or pattern?

4. What are the implications of this decision for the teachers of various subjects?

5. How will this plan be shared with parents and students?

6. How will this decision be evaluated? When?

SAMPLE PATTERN

Grade 6	Grade 7	Grade 8
INTER-DISCIPLINARY/ 2 TEACHERS English Social Studies Mathematics Science Reading	INTER-DISCIPLINARY/ 4 TEACHERS English Social Studies Mathematics Science	INTER-DISCIPLINARY/ 5 TEACHERS English Social Studies Mathematics Science Foreign Language
DISCIPLINARY/ 2 TEACHERS Physical Education	DISCIPLINARY/ 4 TEACHERS Physical Education	DISCIPLINARY/ 2 TEACHERS Physical Education Technology Education Home Economics Art Music
COMBINATION/ 2 TEACHERS Art/Music	COMBINATION/ 6 TEACHERS Art/Music Technology Education/ Home Economics French/Spanish	

4

Role and Function of a Team

Teams all have the same goal — to provide the best possible instructional program for a common group of students. Therefore, it is essential that all teams learn how to work well with each other on a day-to-day basis. Some teams blend quickly; others will need more time and attention. This chapter will suggest an overall format to guide the role and function of a team; the next chapter will describe specific team building activities. All of these activities are suggested to help a group of professionals work efficiently as a team.

WHAT IS A TEAM?

A group of teachers in the process of becoming a teaching team must examine their identity as a team. They can do this by exploring their role and function, extensively at first, and then on a continuing basis as needed.

Team members should be able to determine who they are and why the team exists. Typically, the teachers on a team will have a variety of previous experiences before joining the team situation. They need to explore their commitment to the middle school concept, how they will share responsibilities, and how they will work to support each other before embarking on their adventure as a team. They should know the limits of their local autonomy as a part of a team, a school, and a school district.

Team members need to explore the time commitment they will make. How many team planning periods are provided in the schedule? Will planning time be devoted to team building activities? Will time before and/or after school be needed for team activities?

Another key issue is flexibility. Will the team use flexibility and/or modular scheduling techniques to better meet the unique needs of students? How rigid are the teachers as individuals? To what extent will they have confidence in themselves and their colleagues to develop a meaningful program for their students? How honest will each of them be in communicating with other team members and to other staff members about the team?

The word *team* may have slightly different connotations for students, parents, and teachers. Students have a strong need to identify with something positive during their early adolescent years. They find it difficult to identify with a total school of 1,000 or more, but they can easily identify with a teaching team of 100-140 students. They want to be part of something important and significant; Team 7D or The Explorers can be a very meaningful experience in the life of a student. To wear a T-shirt or a pin with a team logo is an important event that will not be easily forgotten if the experience is positive.

To parents, the term *team* may be a bit more abstract. Most parents did not attend middle schools and do not know the meaning of the term *team*. If a parent has a positive experience in his/her communication with a team, if a child is always talking in positive terms about what happens in school, or if a parent has opportunities to attend orientation meetings, PTA programs, or special events, the parent will readily develop positive feelings about the team concept. If those events are not positive or non-existent, the parent may not truly understand the meaning of the word *team*.

For some teachers, a *team* means team planning while in other cases it may mean actual team teaching. Team planning is an excellent professional growth experience. Team teaching, where the teachers actively teach together, can be an even more enriching experience but is one that should evolve slowly. Teachers must recognize the difference and be comfortable with expectations.

GUIDING THE FUNCTIONING OF A TEAM

Teams of teachers should be given some structure for the functioning of a team. The following planning log, based on Alexander's model for curriculum in the middle school, can provide that structure.

In the category entitled team goal, each team may enter the goal for that team for a week, month, or quarter of the school year. Teams should be goal-oriented; they should identify needs of the students on that team and then work together to meet those needs. Some examples of team goals follow.

Activities will be planned to help students make a smooth adjustment from elementary school to middle school.

All teachers of the team will work together to teach and reinforce three writing skills.

Home base lessons will be devoted to two values education topics — human worth and dignity and integrity.

All teachers will reinforce students' efforts to organize their notebooks.

Teachers will provide extra help at the end of each marking period for students who fail two or more courses.

Teachers will devote one team planning period per week to identify potential correlations within content areas.

Team Planning Log

6A/6B/7A/7B/7C/8A/8B

Week of _____

TEAM GOAL:

_____

_____

Organized knowledge
Skills
Personal development
Pupil adjustment
What we have done to accomplish team goal
Other

Recorder _____

Organized knowledge refers to efforts by the teachers to correlate subject matter between two or more subjects in the interdisciplinary or core/combination subject team. Below are some examples of entries in this section of a planning log.

The English teacher is teaching a novel that is set during the American Revolution. The social studies teacher will devote several lessons to historical background.

The art teacher presents a unit on lettering at the same time the English teacher is presenting a unit entitled "Designs in Art and Poetry." Pupils will submit a project to be evaluated by both teachers.

While the mathematics teacher is teaching a unit on probability and statistics, the science teacher teaches lessons on analyzing data.

The French and social studies teachers teach the concept of revolution concurrently.

The art and music teachers will work together to design the scenery for a musical production.

All correlations need not be by units of instruction. Lessons or even segments of lessons can be correlated to help pupils sense the wholeness of learning.

Teams of teachers frequently find opportunities to correlate skills and use those correlations as the basis for teamwork. One successful practice is to create a "skill-of-the-week" for a team. Typical skills to be included are:

Manuscript form
Setting up a notebook
Reading or listening for main ideas
Use of context clues
Following directions
Putting events in sequential order
Outlining
Reading for details
Skim reading
Use of the card catalog in the library
Reading charts and graphs
Writing complete sentences

Students recognize the importance of those skills when teachers all work together to introduce, reinforce, and evaluate pupil progress in these areas.

The personal development section is the place to record those activities that help the pupil to better understand himself/herself. Usually, these are home base or teacher/advisory activities planned by the team of teachers; but, frequently, teachers utilize suggestions in the curriculum guides of home economics, French, Spanish, or English to work together to help pupils understand the various dimensions of adolescent development.   Examples of personal development activities are:

> Orientation to the new school and to the team
> Decision making activities
> Career development
> Resolving conflict
> Growing up in various cultures
> IALAC (I am Lovable and Capable) activities
> Understanding differences between students
> Helping the handicapped

Ideally, all team members will work together to present personal development activities. Pupils should not perceive that these lessons are the domain of any one teacher.

Teachers should actively care about pupil adjustment. This is one of the major tenets of the middle school philosophy. The team planning log is the place to record the team activities dealing with pupil adjustment without revealing the identity of the student. Entries could be:

> Parent conference(s)
> Team met with pupil
> Guidance counselor attended team meeting to present data about new student
> Special education teacher met with team to review IEP
> Principal met with team to discuss behavior of pupils in cafeteria
> Assistant principal joined team in a meeting with a parent to develop a system of behavior modification for a pupil
> Speech therapist met with team to evaluate a pupil's progress
> Pupil personnel worker met with team to discuss implications of a social history developed after a recent visit to a student's home
> School psychologist visited with team to share information gathered in an educational assessment
> Nurse met with team to discuss pupil with severe handicap

This section of the team planning log must protect the confidentiality of students and parents.

Teams should keep a record of what they do to accomplish the team goal and log the specific items on the weekly planning log. If the team goal were "Activities will be planned to help students make a smooth adjustment from the elementary school to the middle school," the following items could be listed:

> Each student received an individual schedule. An orientation activity was designed to help students learn how to read the schedule.

Students took a tour of the school. On a map of the school, students marked the rooms in which they have classes.

Each student received a copy of the school rules and specific team standards.

The guidance counselor visited the team and gave an overview of the role of the counselor. Slides were used to illustrate several guidance functions within the school. Students learned how to make an appointment with the guidance counselor.

Several home base lessons were devoted to organizing the notebook. Following this, individual teachers reinforced those lessons in the context of their content areas.

Examples of entries in the other or miscellaneous categories would include:

Field trips
Assemblies
Plans for PTA conference night
Meetings with various resource personnel
Planning the administration of standardized tests
Completion of interim reports or report cards
Discussion of homework policies
Planning of registration of students for the next grade

Although this team planning log is most suited for an interdisciplinary or core/combination subject team, it can be useful to guide the single subject team as well. The team planning log can also be the basis for a self-evaluation device to help teams give relatively equal or proportionate amounts of time to the various aspects of their role and function. An example of a self-evaluation process for a team based on the completion of team planning logs over a period of time follows (p. 34).

SUMMARY

It is vital for each team to examine its role and function. This should be done when the team is formed as well as on an as-needed basis. The questions in the Activity (p. 35) are typical of the kinds of questions that need to be answered. Time is needed to respond thoroughly; the structure and rapport that result from the discussions are important to the success of the teaming process.

Assessing Team Planning Logs

DIRECTIONS: Each interdisciplinary team is asked to review the team planning logs submitted for the first quarter and answer the following questions:

1. Approximately what percentage of time in the team meetings has been devoted to correlating content? _____ %

2. How can our team increase the amount of team planning time devoted to correlating content?

3. What skills have we taught through the skill-of-the-week program?

4. What are some skills that we could include during the second quarter?

5. How much time per week do we devote to home base lessons?

6. How many lessons did we do as a team on the values education topic for October?

7. Are we devoting a reasonable amount of team planning time on organized knowledge, skills, and personal development? YES/NO Please explain your answer.

8. Are we devoting a disproportionate amount of time to items listed on the log under the headings of pupil adjustment and other? YES/NO Please explain your answer.

9. What are some possible team goals for the remainder of the school year?

Activity:

After reading this chapter, each team should work together to answer the following questions:

1. What is our primary goal as a team? Where can we post this to constantly remind us of our primary goal?

2. What is our definition of the team process?

3. What is our definition of the middle school concept?

4. What is our professional relationship to each other?

5. What is our relationship to the school as a whole?

6. How much time will we devote to the team process?

7. What is our commitment to the concept of flexibility?

8. How will we attempt to develop a strong, positive team identity among our students and their parents?

9. How do we find out if we are expected to do team teaching as well as team planning?

10. How appropriate is the team planning log in this chapter? What modifications might we make for our team situation?

11. How can we identify opportunities to correlate content and/or skills in our team situation?

12. How can we provide personal development activities for the pupils on our team?

13. How can we utilize the resources to facilitate pupil adjustment?

14. How can we continue to discuss and evaluate our role and function as a team?

5

Activities to
Enhance Team Effectiveness

Once the members of a teaching team are aware of the team's role and function, they are ready for a number of activities designed to enhance team effectiveness. Team building is a process by which persons learn to work effectively to (1) build and maintain a spirit of trust, (2) set and achieve shared goals, and (3) work simultaneously on tasks necessary to the accomplishment of the goals and ultimate maintenance of the team's trustful climate.

Team building activities include (1) getting to know each other, (2) discussing expectations of other team members, (3) discussing expectations of the team leader, (4) discussing expectations of the guidance counselor, administrators, librarian, and other resource personnel, (5) developing procedures to establish team goals, and (6) determining the consensus needed for team decisions. Each of these areas will be explored in this section.

It is important to differentiate between cognitive and affective concerns when talking about team building, communication, and expectations. A cognitive issue is a factual one which is rather obvious such as, "What was your major in college?" or "Who will be the team leader?" Affective concerns are the feelings behind the facts; such feelings are frequently beneath the surface. People may feel uncomfortable about revealing these in such questions as "Why do you object so strongly to that option?" or "What are your fears about working in a team situation?"

GETTING TO KNOW EACH OTHER

It is imperative that team members really get to know each other if the team is to be successful. In many cases, they may have known each other before;

now they will really get to know each other as a result of working closely together. When new middle school faculties are created, teachers who do not know each other are placed on a team. To help teachers get acquainted, the following questions may serve as a guide. Some of the questions are cognitive; others are affective.

1. How long have you taught in this school district?
2. What was your previous teaching assignment?
3. Can you tell us something about your family?
4. What are your hobbies and interests?
5. Are you enrolled in a graduate program?
6. What are your feelings about being a member of this team?
7. What are your feelings about the task of this team?
8. What strengths do you bring to this team?
9. What support do you want from this team?
10. What assumptions have you made about the other members of the team?

It is important for team members to be good listeners as well as to be honest in giving answers. If everyone can be honest, a positive beginning will be achieved.

It is also important to learn how to share. Sharing of prior experiences builds a strong foundation for later sharing when the process is critical to the team's success. Team members must learn to recognize verbal as well as non-verbal cues. More importantly, team members must learn how to handle these cues in ways that are not threatening to each other. The ultimate goal is for team members to feel both comfortable and honest with each other in all circumstances.

EXPECTATIONS OF OTHER TEAM MEMBERS

As part of getting to know each other, team members should begin to discuss their expectations of other team members. Some team members are looking for academic discussions while others are seeking support in handling discipline problems. These expectations must be discussed openly and candidly. Questions to be answered include:

1. What is our schedule of meetings?
2. What are the guidelines for lateness, leaving early, or absenteeism at team meetings?
3. How do we identify organized knowledge topics and skills areas to be correlated?
4. How much time will be spent on home base or teacher/advisory topics?
5. How can we help each other with discipline problems?
6. How will decisions be made?
7. What records of team meetings will be kept?

8. How will we give feedback to each other?
9. How will we evaluate our effectiveness as a team?
10. Are we expected to cooperate on all matters?
11. Is my team relationship more important than the relationship with others in the building? Why?
12. What is it that I really expect from other team members when I have a problem or am upset?
13. How will we work together to establish team goals?

Occasionally, some teams will not jell and their meetings will be little more than occasions for superficial discussions of topics to be recorded on a log for submission to the principal. Most teams, however, will become strong, mutual support systems wherein teachers talk openly and honestly about cognitive as well as affective topics.

EXPECTATIONS OF THE TEAM LEADER

In some school districts, the position of team leader is an appointed position and carries with it a responsibility factor or salary supplement. This person serves as the team leader for the entire year and may be a member of the supervisory team that evaluates teachers.

In other cases, the team leader is appointed by the principal but does not receive any remuneration. In such cases, the team leader is a peer of the teachers and does not serve as an evaluator. A final option is for the team to select its own team leader or even to rotate the position of team leader among all team members during the course of the year.

Obviously, answers to the following questions will differ according to the process of selection used. What needs to happen in all situations, however, is a candid discussion of these questions.

1. What do we expect of the team leader?

2. What does the team leader expect from the members of the team?

3. Who is ultimately responsible for the success of the team?

4. What should the team leader do when there is a deadlock on a particular issue?

5. What should the team leader do when members of the team cannot stay on the topic?

6. Should the team leader delegate tasks to members of the team? Why?

7. What is the relationship between the team leader and the administration of the school?

8. What should team members do when they disagree with the agenda for the team meeting?

9. What should the team leader do when one or more members of the team are silent on a particular subject?

EXPECTATIONS OF RESOURCE PERSONNEL

In addition to developing an excellent working relationship with the other members of the teaching team, team members should utilize other resource personnel effectively. Other resource personnel include the guidance counselor, administrators, librarian, and reading teachers. In addition to focusing on cognitive as well as affective issues, it is important to consider the relationship between the team (as a unit) and "outsiders" who join the team at certain times for certain purposes. Teams should be open to work with resource personnel.

When discussing expectations of teams working with resource persons, it is necessary to consider what the team can do for the resource person as well as what the resource person can do for the team. It is essential that all involved remember the common goal of the entire team process — the improvement of instruction for pupils.

Guidance counselor
1. How often should the guidance counselor attend team meetings?
2. How can the team help the guidance counselor to be more effective?
3. How can the guidance counselor help the team to be more effective?
4. Should the guidance counselor attend all team planning sessions when parents are attending?
5. What is the role of the guidance counselor in planning the skills and personal development programs?
6. What should the guidance counselor do when he/she strongly disagrees with actions or decisions of a team?

Administrators
1. When should the principal attend a team meeting?
2. When should the assistant principal attend a team meeting?
3. What can the administrators do to help the team?
4. How can the team help the administrators?
5. Does the fact that administrators evaluate team members hinder the relationship with the team? Why?

Other resource personnel
1. How can the librarian, reading teacher, and speech therapist become a part of the interdisciplinary teaching process?
2. To what extent should other resource personnel influence team decisions?
3. How can team members help resource personnel do their jobs more effectively?

It is very important for team members to explore their expectations of other team members, the team leader, and various resource personnel who work with the team on a regular basis. As a result, team members should be able to enjoy positive working relationships with each other and various professionals who join the team on occasions.

PROCEDURES TO ESTABLISH TEAM GOALS

Team building activities also include procedures to use in establishing team goals. If all team members work together to create these goals, then they will all work together to achieve them. Goal setting should begin with the total school. Many middle schools establish goals for a school year such as:

> All professional staff members will help to orient new students.
> All teachers will cooperate in implementing various types of teaching teams.
> All teachers will utilize opportunities to teach reading comprehension skills.

These goals are typically the result of assessing the needs of students at the school level.

The middle school organizational plan allows for a similar goal-setting process to occur at the team level. Each team can identify a number of goals that would enable them to grow professionally or respond to the learning needs of students. Typical team goals are:

> Increasing the correlation of content
> More effective assessment of skill activities
> More time devoted to home base activities
> Greater utilization of standardized test scores
> Encouraging students to complete assignments and turn in all work
> Improving notebook organization
> Development of listening skills

Whereas school-wide goals tend to exist for an entire year, team goals could be in effect for several weeks, a month, a quarter, or the entire school year. Teams can establish goals as the need arises. As a team becomes goal oriented, the strength of the team will be more obvious and its effectiveness greatly enhanced.

Activity:

1. What topics or concerns are possible team goals?

2. What choices will we make for team goals?

3. How will we assess our achievement of these goals?

CONSENSUS NEEDED FOR TEAM DECISIONS

Another aspect of team building is determining the consensus needed for team decisions. There are many times when the team needs to make a decision and then support that decision when questioned by a parent, a principal, or a student. Most teams have the autonomy to make certain decisions within areas designated by the administration. Arriving at these decisions should help to unite the team or strengthen the relationship between its members.

Consensus is important because team members must take the time to fully discuss certain points and not let the team leader or one member of the team make the decision. All team members should be encouraged to state their opinions or the reasons for their positions. When there are differences of opinion, team members must take the time to understand the rationale of their colleagues and ultimately to resolve their differences.

Examples of decisions to be made by teams are: whether to change a student from one teaching section to another; whether to take the entire team on a field trip; choosing the skill-of-the-week or the student- of-the-month; choosing a topic and time for a home base activity; drafting guidelines for student behavior; choosing topics in English and social studies that can be correlated; or recommending if a pupil should be promoted to the next grade.

Some issues should require a unanimous decision; others can be resolved by majority vote. What is essential is for team members to determine the majority needed for certain types of situations so they can all ultimately support these decisions. Consensus, again, is needed to build team relationships. If not handled properly, decision making and the lack of support for these decisions can quickly divide a team and hamper its effectiveness.

Activity:

1. What will constitute consensus for our decisions?

2. What will we do when we cannot reach consensus?

3. How will we respond to a team member who cannot support a specific decision?

SUMMARY

Working as members of a team may be a new and/or even difficult experience for many teachers. Teams will not become cohesive automatically. Teachers may need assistance in learning how to work with other teachers on a daily basis.

A number of team building activities were presented in this section. Team members must get to know one another, discuss expectations of other team members, clarify expectations of the team leader and various resource persons who work with the team, develop procedures to establish team goals, and determine the consensus needed for team decisions.

These activities are designed to bring team members closer to each other, enhance team effectiveness, and, ultimately, provide the best possible instructional experience for pupils. Coupled with the structure suggested in the previous chapter, team members should be well on the road to functioning effectively by working through these team building activities so that they will feel secure working as members of a team.

Building a Block-of-Time Master Schedule

Block-of-time scheduling permits two or more teachers of two or more subjects to teach their classes during the same time frame. For example, the English, social studies, mathematics, and science teachers in grade 7 have the same four classes for periods 1 to 5 each day. These teachers are responsible for a total of 250 minutes of instruction for the 110 pupils on the team. In addition to their subject, these instructors may also teach reading, a skills lab, and/or home base advisory during this block-of-time. Their students may be assigned to physical education, art, and music teachers for two periods per day. This allows the interdisciplinary block-of-time teachers to have team and personal planning periods daily.

A second example involves an art and music teacher who have the same 54 students first period each day. The teachers can regroup or subdivide the students however they choose. If all pupils are singing in the chorus, the chorus teacher could form a soprano and an alto group. Sopranos would be in music and art together as one group, and altos would be in another section of music and art. On some days, all 54 pupils could be in chorus; on other days, all 54 pupils could see a film or hear a guest speaker in art. The responsibility for sub-dividing the pupils rests with the teachers involved. No other portion of the schedule is affected once this parallel is created.

Block-of-time scheduling is also a factor in disciplinary or single subject teams. Two mathematics teachers may have 50 pupils for Algebra I third period each day. The same students must be scheduled with the same teachers each day to permit the regrouping of pupils based on their achievement or performance in algebra. In physical education, two teachers may have the same 50 students in an instructional team setting. Grouping and regrouping can be a function of the scope and sequence of the curriculum as well as students' needs.

Some advantages of block-of-time scheduling are:
1. Each teacher can teach his/her primary curriculum area
2. Teachers can correlate content, skills, or personal development activities

3. Time modules can be adjusted by the teachers on the team
4. Pupils can have more time in a certain subject if the situation dictates
5. Time modules can be adjusted to the needs of the pupils
6. Films, guest speakers, and assemblies can be scheduled; yet, each pupil can see each teacher of the team on that day
7. There are no problems with missed classes if all or part of a team is going on a field trip
8. Standardized testing can be scheduled with minimum disruption
9. Longer science laboratory lessons or introductory lessons for new units in all subjects can be scheduled by the team
10. Station teaching can be developed for one or more courses without disruption to the other areas
11. Rotating schedules can be developed for various sections of the team
12. Provision can be made for independent study programs
13. Two or more subjects can be fused together;subjects can be interrelated with broad themes or skills approaches

There is a difference between interdisciplinary team organization and block-of-time. To be an interdisciplinary team, the several teachers do not *have* to be scheduled at the same time. Although it is highly advisable, it is not mandatory. Pure block-of-time requires that the teachers involved are, in fact, teaching the same sections during the same periods of the day. Ideally, all interdisciplinary teams will be scheduled on a block-of-time basis.

7A TEAM SCHEDULE

TIME	PERIOD	MON	TUES	WED	THURS	FRI
8:40-9:30	1	Art/ Music	Physical Education	Physical Education	Explora- tory	Art/ Music
9:30-10:20	2	7A	7A	7A	7A	7A
10:20-11:10	3	7A	7A	7A	7A	7A
11:10-11:40		L	U	N	C	H
11:40-12:30	4	7A	Art/ Music	7A	Art/ Music	7A
12:30-1:20	5	7A	7A	7A	7A	7A
1:20-2:10	6	Explor- atory	7A	7A	7A	7A
2:10-3:00	7	7A	Explora- tory	Art/ Music	Physical Education	Explora- tory

In the above example, the coding 7A indicates that the English, social studies, mathematics, and science teachers are available to teach the four sections of the team. There are 23 periods per week for this pure block-of-time interdisciplinary program.

When the team is assigned to physical education, there are four teachers available to teach them. Pupils may be re-assigned among these four teachers according to skills, needs, or interests because this is a block-of-time disciplinary team.

There are two art and two music teachers available each time the team is scheduled for art/music. A pupil has art one day and music the next day, but other variations are possible because this is a block-of-time core/combination subject team.

During the four exploratory periods, six teachers are available to teach French, Spanish, foods, clothing, wood, and electricity. Pupils rotate among these six stations every six weeks.

6, 7, 8, OR 9 PERIOD DAY

For various reasons, middle schools are organized on a 6, 7, 8, or 9 period day. Some reasons for this decision may be:

Teachers' contract
Staffing guidelines
State curriculum mandates
Local curriculum mandates
Philosophical commitment to the middle school concept
Physical plant limitations
Commitment to block-of-time concept for all subjects
Unique needs of students
Home base advisory program
Intramurals
Extra-curricular activities
Shared campus or teachers with another school
Transportation schedules

In the six period day, or thirty period week, four periods per day can be allocated for the interdisciplinary block of English, social studies, mathematics, and science — providing the flexibility needed for reading and/or advisory experiences. Two periods, or one third of the school day, could be designated for the exploratory program. Using an alternate day schedule, pupils would be enrolled in physical education, art, music, home economics, technology education, and/or computer skills to provide a comprehensive exploratory program. Quarterly rotations could complement the alternate day approach to best balance the distribution of time in these exploratory areas during the entire school year.

More traditionally, a seven period day or thirty-five period week is usually found in middle level schools. This results from the historical development of the junior high school and is an outgrowth of the periods per week charts that allocate a specific amount of time per subject per week. Thus, a typical seven period day or 35 period week may be so organized as indicated below.

Subject	Periods Per Week
English	5
Social Studies	5
Mathematics	5
Science	5
Reading	5
Art	2
Music	3
Physical Education	5
	35

In an effort to be more responsive to the unique needs of middle school students and/or to include subjects prescribed by state, and/or local mandates, many middle schools have moved, or are moving, to an eight period day. The eight period day really needs to be viewed in two perspectives. The first option views the concept of the eight period day as a forty period week with the thrust being to include more subjects in a more formal way for the student. Thus, the following program of studies may reflect a school's effort to provide a better balanced program.

Subject	Periods Per Week
English 8	5
Social Studies 8	5
Mathematics 8	5
Science 8	5
Foreign Language or Reading	5
Physical Education 8	5
Art 8	3
Music 8	3
Home Economics 8/Technology 8	3
Advisory	1
	40

In the other scenario, the eight period day is used to expand the seven period day as needed to be flexible and responsive to student needs. Specifically, in addition to the traditional seven periods per day, an eighth module could be added for an advisory program, a free reading experience called DEAR (Drop Everything and Read), mentoring, skills instruction, or music rehearsals. The additional module need not be for the same amount of time as the other periods. Thus, a flexible eight period day might be organized in the following fashion:

8:40- 9:15	ADVISORY
9:15-10:00	Period 1
10:00-10:45	Period 2
10:45-11:30	Period 3
11:30-12:15	Period 4
12:15-12:45	LUNCH
12:45- 1:30	Period 5
1:30- 2:15	Period 6
2:15- 3:00	Period 7

Just as the eight period day was an alternative to or extension of the seven period day, the nine period day may be viewed as an alternative to or an extension of the eight period day. One option, obviously, is to divide the school day into nine equal portions which would allow students to enroll in nine separate courses. The other option is to operate on a forty period week to achieve the eight period day but utilize a modular ninth period extension for home base or free reading as needed.

In making a decision to utilize a 6, 7, 8, or 9 period day, a number of factors must be considered. Of primary importance are the needs of early adolescent learners. Flexibility must be viewed as a means toward that end. Unique state and local mandates must be satisfied. Ultimately, decisions must reflect the totality of the curriculum and the extent to which both structure and flexibility are involved on a daily basis.

CREATING A BLOCK-OF-TIME SCHEDULE

The master schedule becomes the vehicle to implement the various philosophical aspects of the effective middle level school. Program elements such as team teaching, a curriculum with a strong emphasis on skill development, the teacher/advisory program, and special activities will not be able to achieve their true potential unless the necessary accommodations are made in the master schedule. In most secondary schools, the master schedule is created during the summer months by the principal and/or assistant principals. In the effective middle level school, it is desirable for team leaders to have an active role in the design of the schedule. In fact, the basic schedule can be completed before teachers leave for their summer vacations.

In the effective middle level school, the master schedule is an overall outline that permits flexible and modular scheduling strategies. Individual teaching teams may subdivide their 250 minutes into six or seven modules so that students might have a reading program and home base activities in addition to classes in English, social studies, mathematics, science, and French. Teams may decide to rotate the sequence so that all teaching sections have the advantages and/or disadvantages of having a particular subject first or last period each day. There could be four or five variations of the team schedule. Classes could even meet at different times each month.

In the example below, the schedule features a seven period day. Lunch is a 30 minute module of time between periods three and four, four and five, or five and six.

BELL SCHEDULE

Homeroom -   8:30- 8:40
Period 1 -   8:40- 9:30
Period 2 -   9:30-10:20
Period 3 -   10:20-11:10

"A" LUNCH	"B" LUNCH"	"C" LUNCH
Lunch -11:10-11:40	Pd. 4 - 11:10-12:00	Pd. 4 - 11:10-12:00
Pd. 4 - 11:40-12:30	Lunch - 12:00-12:30	Pd. 5 - 12:00-12:50
Pd. 5 - 12:30- 1:20	Pd. 5 - 12:30- 1:20	Lunch - 12:50- 1:20

Period 6 -   1:20 - 2:10
Period 7 -   2:10 - 3:00

STEPS IN BUILDING A SCHEDULE

1. **Determine the program of studies for each grade level**
   The first step in building a schedule involves delineating the program of studies for each grade level. Specific courses must be listed along with the number of periods per week the course is offered. Exploratory courses as well as electives should be available for student selection. In deciding periods per week, consideration must be given to possible teaming options or the clustering of courses.

GRADE 6		GRADE 7	
Subject	Periods per week	Subject	Periods per week
Lang. Arts/Reading	10	English	5
Social Studies	5	Social Studies	5
Mathematics	5	Mathematics	5
Science	5	Science	5
Physical Education	5	Physical Education	5
Art	2	Art	2
Music	3	Music	3
	35	Technology Education/ Home Economics/ Foreign Language/ Exploratory	5
			35

GRADE 8

Subject	Periods per Week
English	5
Social Studies	5
Mathematics	5
Science	5
French I, Spanish I, or Reading Skills	5
Art	2
Music	2
Technology Education/Home Economics	3
Physical Education	3
	35

2. Make the necessary decisions on teaming arrangements

There are three approaches to team teaching in the middle school — interdisciplinary, disciplinary, and core/combination. The three approaches are not mutually exclusive; an overall plan for instruction could involve all three approaches.

Additionally, decisions must be made on the number of teachers per team. Teams could consist of two, three, four, or five members. The special education program should be interactive with the teaming configuration. Finally, consideration must be given to the exploratory subjects. Art, music, technology education, home economics, foreign language, and physical education teachers can and should be involved in the teaming process.

Administrators must find ways to actively involve all teachers in some form of teaching team to achieve the full potential of the middle school. Patterns should be created to reflect the total organization of grades 6 through 8. These patterns should reflect the developmental characteristics of students. A sample pattern follows.

GRADE 6	GRADE 7	GRADE 8
Interdisciplinary/ **2 Teachers** English Social Studies Mathematics Science Science Reading	**Interdisciplinary/** **2 Teachers** English Social Studies Mathematics	**Interdisciplinary/** **3 Teachers** English Social Studies Foreign Language
Disciplinary/ **2 Teachers** Physical Education	**Disciplinary/** **2 Teachers** Physical Education	**Disciplinary/** **2 Teachers per** **subject** Mathematics Science Art Music Physical Education Technology Education Home Economics
Core/Combination **2 Teacher** Art/Music	**Core/Combination** **6 Teachers** Art/Music Technology Education/ Home Economics/ Foreign Language	

3. Create a preliminary registration form

The preliminary registration form may be all that is needed for a manual scheduling process, but for a computerized system it is only an intermediate form before pupils complete computerized scan sheets. The preliminary registration form can reflect the decisions made on team teaching as well as the course numbers that are vital for computer scheduling and the automated grade reporting system.

Preliminary Registration for Grade 6

COURSE	PLACEMENT
READING 6	All students are to take a Reading course. The following is recommended for your student: _____ Basic Reading 6 -7401 _____ Reading 6 -7402 _____ G & T Reading 6 -7405 _____ Sp. Ed. Reading 6 -7408
LANGUAGE ARTS 6	All students are to take a Language Arts course. The following is recommended for your student: _____ Basic Language Arts 6 -0811 _____ Language Arts 6 -0812 _____ G & T Language Arts 6 -0815 _____ Sp. Ed. Language Arts 6 -0818

COURSE	PLACEMENT
SOCIAL STUDIES 6	All students are to take a Social Studies course. The following is recommended for your student: _____ Basic Social Studies 6 -0821 _____ Social Studies 6 -0822 _____ G & T Social Studies 6 -0825 _____ Sp. Ed. Social Studies 6 -0828
MATHEMATICS 6	All students are to take a Mathematics course. The following is recommended for your student: _____ Basic Mathematics 6 -0831 _____ Mathematics 6 -0832 _____ G & T Mathematics 6 -0835 _____ Sp. Ed. Mathematics 6 -0838
SCIENCE 6	All students are to take a Science course. The following is recommended for your student: _____ Basic Science 6 -0841 _____ Science 6 -0842 _____ G & T Science 6 -0845 _____ Sp. Ed. Science 6 -0848
PHYSICAL EDUCATION 6	All students are to take a Physical Education course The following is recommended for your student: _____ Physical Education 6 -0900 _____ Adaptive Phys Ed 6 -7150
ART 6	All students are to take an Art course. The following is recommended for your student: ___ Art 6 -0850
MUSIC 6	All students are to take a Music course. The following is recommended for your student: _____ Music 6 -0860 _____ Chorus 6 -0890 _____ Percussion 6 -0872 _____ Woodwind 6 -0873 _____ Brass 6 -0876 _____ Strings 6 -0877

4. Determine the grouping procedures

It is important to involve the administration and faculty in determining grouping procedures. Overall, there are many benefits to having each teaching team as a heterogeneous group; each team would have pupils of various ability levels. This helps to enhance the self-concept of all pupils and teams.

Specific teaching sections can be organized on a homogeneous, contiguous, or heterogeneous basis depending on the local philosophy. In situations calling for a combination of homogeneous and heterogeneous grouping, teams should be paralleled.

Using these parallels, cross-team regrouping can be utilized so that students could be in reading/language arts classes based on reading scores, in mathematics classes according to mathematics levels, and heterogeneously grouped for social studies and science.

The master schedule can be constructed to facilitate these important issues for early adolescent students. The scheduling of special education students should be considered at this point in the scheduling process.

5. Conduct the registration of students

Pupils, under the direction of the faculty or staff, complete the final registration form if they are on a computerized system. Teachers or guidance counselors enter the fourth digit to indicate grouping decisions. Thus, the data are loaded into the registration file. One of the products is a profile of each individual student. In some cases, additional digits can be added for team designation, teaching section within that team, and/or homeroom section.

6. Analyze the student request tally sheet

A tally must be developed, manually or by the computer, indicating the number of pupils enrolled in each course. In summarizing the enrollment for subjects, the fourth digit becomes very significant. For example,

> 7401-Basic Reading 6
> 7402-Reading 6
> 7405-Gifted and Talented Reading 6
> 7408-Special Education Reading 6

In essence, each rating is a different course for enrollment purposes. The student registration tally sheet can become the basis for organizing the school for teaming and instruction. Data can be grouped by grade, department, and/or team. Teachers' assignments are created in light of these data. A sample tally sheet follows.

STUDENT REQUEST TALLY - GRADE 6		
Course Name	**Course Code**	**Enrollment**
Reading 6	7401	25
	7402	200
	7405	47
	7408	18
		Total 290
Language Arts 6	0811	25
	0812	200
	0815	47
	0818	18
		Total 290
Social Studies 6	0821	17
	0822	207
	0825	54
	0828	12
		Total 290

Course Name	Course Code	Enrollment
Mathematics 6	0831	30
	0832	177
	0835	62
	0838	_21
		Total 290
Science 6	0841	17
	0842	207
	0845	54
	0848	_12
		Total 290
Physical Education 6	0900	275
Adaptive Physical Education	7150	_15
		Total 290
Art 6	0850	290
Music 6	0860	40
Chorus 6	0890	120
Percussion 6	0872	21
Woodwind 6	0873	41
Brass 6	0876	44
Strings 6	0877	_24
		Total 290

7. Study the conflict charts

Conflict charts need to be created (manually or by the computer) to determine patterns or combinations of courses in which pupils have enrolled. For example, a sixth grader with several G & T courses may take any of six music electives. It is essential, then, that all six options be available.

This is important in building the master schedule as well as in assigning pupils to teams. Each pupil must be placed properly for each of the required as well as elective courses. Conflict charts help to determine which pupils will be assigned to certain teaching teams to permit the full potential of the teaming process.

A conflict chart can be developed for each course. This matrix reveals the other courses taken by the students. For example, 35 students are enrolled in Gifted and Talented English 8, nineteen are also enrolled in French I, 16 are enrolled in Spanish I, and all but five of the students are enrolled in G & T Social Studies 8.

CONFLICT LISTING		
1025	G & T English Grade 8	- 35
1480	French I Grade 8	- 19
1800	Spanish I Grade 8	- 16
2022	Social Studies 8	- 5
2025	G & T Social Studies 8	- 30
2510	Art Grade 8	- 29
2515	G & T Art 8	- 6
3023	Mathematics 8	- 1
3120	Algebra I Grade 8	- 3
3250	G & T Math 8	- 31
4062	General Science Grade 8	- 5
4065	G & T Science Grade 8	- 30
6310	General Music Grade 8	- 11
6350	Chorus Grade 8	- 15

8. Decide the composition of teams

Teachers need to be involved in designing and confirming the blueprint for composition of teams at each grade level. All factors or decisions made to this point must be reflected in this process. Pupils of various ability levels should be properly distributed among teams. All pupils, regardless of their ability levels, should be placed in the elective of their choice. Interdisciplinary and exploratory teams must be interactive within the schedule to enhance students' needs, the middle school concept, and the variety of team approaches to instruction.

9. Write the table of teachers' assignments

Most school districts require that the building principal submit a table of teacher assignments to the superintendent as part of the organizational plan for the forthcoming year. This table will detail the specific assignments for each teacher.

For example, Mr. Jones will teach Social Studies 7 to 118 pupils for a 25 period per week block-of-time, have three team planning periods per week, have two lunch duties per week, and have five duty-free periods per week as required by the teaching contract. This table should then become a useful tool in developing the master schedule, not just a report for an external source.

10. Develop a tentative schedule by placing courses on daily/ weekly schedules by teams

Team leaders and department heads should be involved in the actual construction of the schedule. They will be available to make certain decisions about blocks-of-time and then will be able to explain why certain decisions were or were not made.

Using a mosaic approach, the following sub-steps are suggested in developing the master schedule for a sixth grade team. In each case, the teachers are scheduled on a parallel basis. The pattern described is repeated for each team. A record must be kept of the decisions made for special area teachers because they teach more than one team of students.

a. Place the art/music core/combination subject team (two art and two music teachers) on the grid. All pupils of a given team should go to art or music at the same times. In this example, 110 students could be assigned to two art and two music teachers. One of the music teachers could be an instrumental specialist while the other could handle either vocal or general music. Students would go to art one day and music the next. Pupils could be regrouped between these four teachers.

b. Place the physical education team (four teachers) on the grid. All pupils of a given team will go to physical education at the same time.

c. Remainder of the time (25 periods) is devoted to the interdisciplinary team consisting of teachers for English, social studies, science, and mathematics. Each teacher teaches that subject to all four sections of the team on a rotating basis. Students have each subject at least 1 period per day.

d. For those periods designated as reading, the four teachers are joined by two additional professionals so that the team of 110 students can be regrouped according to reading levels. Thus, each interdisciplinary team teacher teaches one period of reading in addition to the four periods of the subject specialty. By adding two additional professionals for the reading program, class size is significantly reduced.

e. Using course numbers and section numbers, this information must then be encoded into the computer for storage purposes.

Interdisciplinary teams can schedule team planning periods when students are in art/music or physical education. Art/music and physical education teams can have team planning periods when students are with their interdisciplinary cluster of teachers. Obviously, it is not possible for all teachers to meet while the students are in school. By using creative, flexible approaches to the teachers' work day, times can be arranged prior to the arrival or after the dismissal of students for all teachers of a given team to convene.

6A TEAM SCHEDULE

PERIOD	MON	TUES	WED	THURS	FRI
1	6A	6A	Reading	Reading	Physical Education
2	Reading	Art/ Music	Art/ Music	6A	Art/ Music
3	Art/ Music	Reading	Physical Education	Art/ Music	6A
	L	U	N	C	H
4	6A	Phys Education	6A	Physical Education	6A
5	6A	6A	6A	6A	Reading
6	6A	6A	6A	6A	6A
7	Physical Education	6A	6A	6A	6A

11. Assign pupils to teams

By this point in the process, the computer is storing information about the courses requested by each student as well as the times these courses are available according to the tentative schedule developed. The initial run of the computer identifies the number of students who can successfully be assigned to teams and full schedules, the number that cannot be fully assigned, and the reasons why those not assigned could not be assigned to teams.

Manually, pupils can be assigned to teams according to academic levels, electives, and the balancing of classes by sex and race. If a student is not easily assigned, some adjustment can be identified. By the end of the process, each pupil should be assigned to a team, be properly placed academically, and enrolled in the elective requested.

12. Analyze the loading process/assignment of pupils to teams

Whether the initial assignment of pupils to teams was manual or by computer, there needs to be a careful assessment of the placement process. Were any students' programs incomplete? Why did some classes fill while others did not? How balanced are the pupil loads of teachers in the various departments? Is each student in the proper grouping for each course?

13. Make adjustments to original schedule

As a result of the analysis of the loading process and the initial assignment of pupils to teams, it may be necessary to make adjustments to the original schedule. The capacity of certain sections may need to be adjusted; additional sections of art, music, physical education, or technology education may be created to accommodate the team structure. Certain pupils may alter their requests for electives. As a result, it is likely that there will be changes in the master schedule. These changes should be made before the schedule is run again.

14. Request additional run(s) of the master schedule
An advantage of the computerized scheduling process is the opportunity to run the schedule more than once. After the adjustments to the original schedule are made, additional runs are needed until 100% of the students are placed in their courses and classes are balanced.

15. Assign homeroom sections within teams and/or grade level
Pupils on a team should be assigned to homerooms on a heterogeneous/alphabetical order basis. The teachers of the interdisciplinary team can serve as homeroom and/or home base teachers.

16. Publish necessary lists
Teachers should have class lists for various groupings within the interdisciplinary team subjects as well as art/music, physical education, reading, exploratory, technology education, and home economics classes.

17. Orient teachers and students to the master schedule
If teachers are expected to make maximum use of blocks-of-time and parallels that exist in the schedule, they must understand how the schedule was constructed and options that exist. It is also important that pupils understand the schedule for their team. This is typically accomplished as part of orientation programs at the beginning of the school year.

Activity:

1. Who is responsible for constructing the master schedule?

2. What other staff members have the opportunity to participate in the process?

3. What guidelines does the school district provide for building the master schedule?

4. What local options does the school have?

5. What data do we need to gather in preparation for building a master schedule?

6. What is the time chronology for building the schedule?

7. How will the faculty learn about the schedule so that various teaching teams can begin to function?

8. How will the effectiveness of the master schedule be evaluated?

7

Including Special
Education Within the Team

A discussion of building a block-of-time master schedule as a means of implementing the team process in the middle school would be incomplete without including concerns or needs of handicapped students. This chapter discusses ways to include special education within the team process in the middle school. Teaming can play a vital role in facilitating the success of handicapped students at this fragile stage of their development. Although certain curriculum topics will be presented, the focus is on delivering that curriculum to best meet the unique learning needs of early adolescent special needs students. The real issue is how to make handicapped students, teachers of special education classes, and parents of special education students feel worthwhile and included in the mainstream of the middle school experience.

WHAT ARE THE ISSUES?

1. **Inclusion versus exclusion.** Educators contend that they want to include special needs students in the total school process or organization, but the schedule frequently makes a very different statement. Too often, these students are excluded from the mainstream when the scheduling process is analyzed. The problem is that those responsible for constructing the master schedule do not know how to successfully include students requiring special education courses in the totality of the teaming process.

2. **All students have special needs.** Rather than identifying ways that special education students are different from other students and thereby rationalizing exclusion, those responsible for organizing the middle school for effective instruction should take a broader approach. Every student is an individual, and thus every middle school student has special needs. The

team approach to instruction increases the opportunities both to delineate the uniqueness of each early adolescent and manage the instructional process to address those uniquenesses.

3. **Self-concept.** The ultimate goal of middle level education is to enhance students' self-concepts. Middle school educators must do more than pay lip service to this goal; they must become more sensitive to the effects of a schedule on the self-concept of students with special needs. Part of the problem results from not assessing the self-concept issue thoroughly; the other portion of the problem involves breaking away from traditional, rigid patterns of scheduling that inhibit personality development.

4. **Determining the best approach for children with educational handicaps and/or disabilities.** There are a number of approaches; yet administrators are either not informed about or able to utilize the variety of organizational techniques available at the middle school level. Research provides no conclusive answer, so educators should examine factors and elements associated with facilitating student success. Administrators should be encouraged to assess the full spectrum of options.

5. **Making the schedule work to the advantage of special education.** Special education programs depend upon the scheduling mechanism to be effective. With adequate planning, analysis of data, and experimentation with possibilities, schedules will be more successful for students with special needs.

6. **Making the schedule adequately flexible.** The schedule will be flexible and interactive if those building the schedule are creative in arranging parallels. Parallels are needed so that pupils can be in regular education and/or special education classes at the same times. Problems with parallels result when too many classes need to be aligned with each other. Larger middle schools have more opportunities for flexibility.

7. **Making the team process facilitate learning for special needs students.** Students with special needs are vital parts of each school and team. Recognizing the dignity and worth of every student calls for special needs students to be integral parts of teams. Within the team, all middle school students must be viewed on an individual basis, each with particular strengths and needs. Plans for instruction should be developed accordingly.

8. **Curriculum.** Aspects of the curriculum issue must be addressed from the perspective of scheduling. Is curriculum for the special needs student the same as or different from the regular education program? When do handicapped students need a truly functional curriculum rather than or in addition to an adapted curriculum? If a student is in a special education program with a functional curriculum, what happens when that individual is deemed ready for the regular curriculum? Obviously, these questions need to be answered in each school or district.

9. **Cooperation between special education and regular education teachers.** The schedule of classes for students is just one part of the organizational process. The schedule must provide a time for special and regular education teachers to meet on a regular, systematic basis. Working together, they can monitor the performance of students. For example, the special education teacher may assess the performance of a mainstreamed student or help the regular education teacher prepare for a student to be placed in the near future. Problems arise if these focus meetings do not occur during the regular work day.

LEAST RESTRICTIVE ENVIRONMENT

In studying the Regular Education Initiative (REI), Baltimore County (Maryland) Public Schools developed a position paper entitled "Least Restrictive Environment" (1989). The goal was to change the perspective that every student receiving special education services had to be considered "a special education student." Rather, the purpose of LRE was to help educators see programs and services of special education as available along with all other programs and services for middle school students. Attention should be called to the type of instructional program and service rather than to the label on the student. Therefore, all students are in regular classes except when receiving special instructional services. In summary, the least restrictive environment concept suggests that to the maximum extent possible handicapped children are to be educated along with children who are not handicapped. This has major implications for organizing the middle school for instruction and, more specifically, for building the master schedule to meet the needs of all students.

Advantages of least restrictive environment identified in the report included:

Extension of recognition of the school's responsibility for all students. Each middle school was to become more aware of the responsibility to organize the school so that all students are placed in the least restrictive environment.

Less separation of special education from general education. With the implementation of this program, more opportunities will be identified for students to mix with each other.

Flexible use of all teachers to provide a continuum of services. Ultimately, more teachers in the building will be working with special education students. This focus on a variety of personnel and services will enable each student to be placed appropriately for each period. Regular education teachers will have more opportunities for interaction with teachers of special needs students.

Improved classroom instruction. Students will benefit when a wide variety of approaches are used to deliver the curriculum. Teachers will become more proficient in providing and evaluating instruction.

Improved curricular offerings. Students with special needs will have a greater opportunity for a variety of courses and experiences.

Increased instructional efficiency as a result of the team process. With proper training, teaching teams will become more efficient in delivering instruction. Other types of teams focusing on student needs may also become more important. For example, the Admissions, Review, and Dismissal unit of the pupil services division of the school will become even more important in managing instruction.

More effective scheduling of students. As teachers, counselors, and administrators learn to implement LRE, the scheduling process will become more precise in responding to needs of students. Through teaming and parallels, there will be more opportunities for placement and interactive schedules. Through pilot experiences, scheduling options will increase.

Improved self-image and achievement for all students. Obviously, the major purpose of LRE is to enhance self-image and expand opportunities for student achievement. Although schools will need training and time to become successful in this venture, the benefits to students will justify the investment.

Clearly, there are barriers to the successful implementation of LRE. In many cases, special education practices have become so entrenched that it is believed they are required by law. More flexibility exists than many educators realize. To move in the direction of integrating special and regular education, educators need a full understanding of the intent of LRE, training for general education teachers to work with special needs students, experience in combining the two programs, and a definite structure to provide support for the concept of differentiating instruction for all students.

Central office personnel should play a major part in implementing LRE. Instructional offices should implement a consortium concept for curriculum development, implementation, and evaluation. Support personnel from the area of special education should work with each subject supervisor and be available to help classroom teachers. In writing curriculum, special and regular education teachers should work together to design strategies that will ensure special needs students will be successful. Inservice courses and summer workshops are needed to help all teachers move in this direction. General and special education supervisors should visit classrooms to assess the extent to which this program is successful.

A major thrust of staff development should be to help all teachers recognize commonalities in teaching all students. Ultimately, teachers should be prepared to instruct students with a range of achievement levels and needs. The delivery of special services should be determined by the students' instructional needs rather than a handicapping label.

MODELS OF ORGANIZATION

As middle schools begin to incorporate special education within the team approach, various organizational models emerge. All middle schools should provide the least restrictive environment. However, schools will need time to accomplish this goal. They will need to explore various options and develop models for students who are not capable of functioning in a regular classroom. Four major models for organizing middle schools to include special education within the team approach are presented in this chapter. Schools will need to decide which model or models to use in light of the uniqueness of that situation.

1. Interactive, parallel model
In this model, students are placed in regular education and/or special education classes according to their Individualized Educational Programs (IEP). Students may be placed in special education classes for three or four subjects and in regular education classes for the complement of their program. The objective, obviously, is for the scheduling process to have parallels which permit interaction in an effort to meet the needs of students.

To accomplish this model, Team 6A may consist of two regular education teachers and one special education teacher whose schedules are paralleled as follows:

PERIOD	REGULAR TEACHER #1	REGULAR TEACHER #2	SPECIAL TEACHER #1
1		Reading/Language Arts	
2			
3	Social Studies	Science	Social /Studies/ Science
4			
5		Mathematics	
6		Team Planning	
7		Personal Planning	

A majority of the students assigned to this team are in regular education and will spend all of their time with regular education teachers. Some of the students may require special education placement in all areas and will be exclusively and individually assigned to the special education teacher. The benefit of this schedule is that a student may be assigned to some special education and some regular education classes; thus, the student moves interactively among the three teachers. Placement in special education classes is a function of analyzing the student's goals on the Individualized Educational Program (IEP). Parent involvement is essential in this goal-setting process. Teachers can, however, be extremely involved in modifying the IEP according to the student's growth and progress. The level of service required by the IEP determines the ratio of special to regular education classes. The Admission, Review, Dismissal (ARD) team process is the mechanism by which placement decisions are made.

For example, a student's goals on the IEP may require special education placement in reading/language arts and social studies with regular placement in mathematics and science. Another situation may call for special education placement in reading/language arts with all other classes in regular education. Students who progress can be moved from a special education class to a regular education class according to guidelines in that district.

Teachers must have common team planning time to achieve both curriculum integration and proper placement decisions. Without this time for professional collaboration, the goals of the program cannot be accomplished. The regular education teacher must be prepared to receive a handicapped student; the special education teacher must be in a position to follow-up on the success of a student. In this model, all special needs students must be placed on a team that is parallel and interactive.

For a five subject interdisciplinary team, special education teachers could be assigned on a parallel basis to the five teachers responsible for English, social studies, mathematics, science, and foreign language. There are five subjects, five regular teaching sections, and five regular education teachers on this team. The special education teachers have a schedule that is parallel to teaching section "C".

PERIOD

A	English
B	Social Studies
C	Mathematics/Special Education Parallel
D	Science
E	Foreign Language

PERIOD

A	Social Studies
B	Mathematics
C	Science/Special Education Parallel
D	Foreign Language
E	English

PERIOD

A	Mathematics
B	Science
C	Foreign Language/Special Education Parallel
D	English
E	Social Studies

PERIOD

A	Science
B	Foreign Language
C	English/Special Education Parallel
D	Social Studies
E	Mathematics

PERIOD

A	Foreign Language
B	English
C	Social Studies/Special Education Parallel
D	Mathematics
E	Science

To maximize opportunities for mainstreaming, the section designated as "C" should begin with a smaller student census than the other four sections. Students can be grouped on a homogeneous or heterogeneous basis in this model. Special needs students can ultimately be placed in all five regular education courses if the IEP so indicates.

2. Regular education/special education cooperative teaching

In response to the Regular Education Initiative, special education students may receive instruction in regular education classes. To accomplish this goal, special and regular education teachers co-teach a class that consists of both categories of students. In some ways, this is similar to the single subject team teaching model. One teacher is the lead teacher; the other, a co-teacher. Special education students capable of handling such an assignment are assigned to these classes; others are assigned to a self-contained class of special needs students.

In the following example, a special education teacher may teach two subjects to minimize planning as well as the number of special education teachers needed within the building for this model to operate. A student's schedule may be developed from the following master schedule:

Period 1 -	English -	Regular Education English Teacher + Special Education Teacher #1
Period 2 -	Social Studies -	Regular Education Social Studies Teacher + Special Education Teacher #1
Period 3 -	Mathematics - Regular Education Mathematics Teacher + Special Education Teacher #2	
Period 4 -	Science - Regular Education Science Teacher + Special Education Teacher #2	
Period 5 -	Physical Education	
Period 6 -	Art/Music	
Period 7 -	Technology Education/Home Economics/Computers/ Foreign Language Exploratory	

During periods 5, 6, and 7, students are integrated with regular education students and teachers. Another variation of this model features the same regular education teacher teaching both language arts and social studies and teaming with a special education teacher for these subjects. In an eight period day, these two teachers could co-teach three groups for two periods each and then have time for team and personal planning.

The success of this model depends upon a commitment to realistic class size, staff development for teachers, and the careful selection of teachers who can work together. It is critical that students view both teachers as equals and that teachers view themselves as partners in this venture. Implementing this model facilitates regrouping of students. Teachers selected for this assignment must have the ability to plan for a variety of modalities of learning and evaluation. They will need strong support from the administration, other staff members, parents, and community for this model to succeed.

In piloting this model, schools may choose to schedule students of varying cognitive abilities so that handicapped students have the opportunity to work with their non-handicapped peers. Ultimately, all students benefit. In adopting this model, schools should begin with a pilot project with one team or just one grade level. Guidelines should be created for the role of lead teacher and co-teacher, although all teachers should have the opportunity to serve in each capacity. Summer workshops would be an ideal opportunity to train teachers in the necessary skills. During the school year, teachers involved could go on a retreat to evaluate and update the model.

3. Parallels for self-contained classes

Some special needs students should have a self-contained setting to maximize their opportunities for success. If a middle school has two sections of students with learning disabilities, these two sections may be scheduled on a parallel basis so the two special education teachers may have opportunities for team teaching and exchanges. Both teachers would get to know all students and have the opportunity for some subject matter specialization.

Period	Teacher #1	Teacher #2
1	Reading	Reading
2	Language Arts	Mathematics
3	Social Studies	Science
4	Language Arts	Mathematics
5	Social Studies	Science
6	Team Planning	Team Planning
7	Personal Planning	Personal Planning

Using a block-of-time schedule, teachers may group and regroup students to capitalize on strengths of teachers and maximize opportunities for student interaction. Rooms of the two teachers should be adjacent, and adequate time should be allocated for the planning process.

In some schools, there may be a self-contained program for children with learning disabilities and another program for students with both learning disabilities and emotional problems. If these teachers were scheduled on a parallel basis, full benefit of the least restrictive environment concept could be achieved.

To enhance student mobility and fluidity of program, it is also desirable to parallel a regular education class to the classes for pupils with learning disabilities and emotional problems. This arrangement allows for a full continuum of services and permits the program to meet the unique needs of each student. Maximum potential for appropriate placement exists. Staff development and follow-up studies would enable the faculty to realize the outcomes of their efforts.

4. Resource room concept

Resource rooms provide extra help for students in any academic area, or the resource room teacher can serve as a consultant to any teacher in the building. Student needs determine the quantity and nature of service. This approach is in addition to, not in place of special services. Operated by special education teachers, instruction is available in any academic area to reinforce the regular curriculum. Teachers may receive assistance in modifying and/or adapting curriculum for pupils in regular education who have atypical learning styles. Study skills and counseling support are included. Teachers identify alternate teaching and learning strategies for this special needs population. Not a separate course, the scheduling process becomes very fluid or elastic. Students might attend this program for specific units of study or skill areas within a specific course. A typical student schedule in an eight period day might be:

Period	Schedule
1	English
2	Social Studies
3	Mathematics
4	Science
5	Resource Room
6	Art/Music
7	Physical Education
8	Technology Education/Home Economics

SUMMARY

Special needs students must be included within the overall team approach to instruction in the middle grades. In the final analysis, success is dependent upon the commitment to:

On-going assessment of the developmental needs of each student

The middle school concept for all students

Interdisciplinary approaches to the delivery of curriculum

A continuum of services

Maximum interaction of special needs and regular education students

Staff development for all teachers

Flexible, interactive schedules

Time for team planning

Related services such as speech/language, occupational therapy, and physical therapy are easily incorporated into each of these models depending on the nature and severity of the student's handicap.

Activity:

1. To what extent is our school now including special education students within the team approach?

2. What scheduling method(s) are currently used for special needs students? How effective are these current methods?

3. How do the efforts of this school align with REI and LRE?

4. What is the long range goal of this school in terms of including special education within the team approach?

5. What staff development is needed to reach that long range goal?

6. How do we become more proficient in modifying or adapting curriculum and instructional strategies for students with various handicapping conditions?

7. Which of the four models could possibly be used in this school?

8. How will the efforts of the school to include special education within the team approach be evaluated?

8

Effective Use
of Planning Periods

Teaching teams need several periods per week for planning purposes. Without common planning periods, it is virtually impossible for clusters of teachers to be effective. These team planning periods should be part of the regular work day and should not be taken from duty-free periods that may be guaranteed by the teacher contract.

Teaching teams may have as many as five planning periods per week. Obviously, the more periods for team planning the more productive that team can be. Administrators and supervisors must gear their expectations of a team's accomplishments to the number of periods available in the master schedule for meetings. Teachers must realize too that team planning time is a part of their regular work day and that they are professionally accountable for the best use of the time.

RELATIONSHIP BETWEEN PLANNING PERIODS
AND THE INSTRUCTIONAL PROGRAM

There is a direct correlation between the utilization of planning periods and effectiveness of the instructional program. Almost all that happens in a team teaching situation results from plans developed during planning periods.

For example, if an interdisciplinary team is planning to teach a skill-of-the-week such as reading for main ideas in English, social studies, mathematics, and science classes, all necessary procedures must be arranged during team planning periods. Or, if a physical education team would like to regroup pupils for a gymnastics unit so that more experienced pupils could be in one group while novices were divided between the other two instructors, the regrouping process would need to be arranged during a team planning period.

Teachers need to recognize the close relationship between planning periods and the instructional program. To do this, they need to:

Examine their own course of study to identify opportunities for team teaching — content, skills, and personal development

Share with teachers of other subjects those topics and skills that can be correlated as part of the regular instructional program and which would enhance the learning experiences of the pupils

Prepare a calendar so these unified learning experiences can be scheduled throughout the school year

Utilize team planning periods to arrange for special activities such as field trips, films, and guest speakers to reinforce common learning experiences and/or to serve as culminating activities

Arrange a calendar of teacher-made tests and standardized tests to carefully evaluate pupil progress and attainment of goals.

Without planning periods, the team process will simply not occur. But even with common planning time, efforts must be expended to insure appropriate use of these periods. A number of suggestions designed to make the planning periods effective are included in this chapter.

GROUP DYNAMICS

Group dynamics play a major role in the proper use of planning periods. The interaction of forces within groups as they work to achieve their objectives is the focal point of group dynamics. Needs of individuals should become subordinate to group needs. Unfortunately, this is not always the case. In group situations, certain roles and processes can be anticipated. Benne and Sheets (1966) listed various roles played by individuals in group situations. Some of these are:

Initiator-coordinator who suggests a new view of the problem

Information seeker who asks for facts and clarification

Opinion seeker who is primarily interested in opinions of others

Information giver who provides objective data

Opinion giver who states his/her view of the problem

Elaborator who expands the given data and attempts to show how matters will evolve

Coordinator who clarifies and integrates ideas

Orienter who attempts to locate the position and direction of the group

Evaluator-critic who evaluates progress according to logic

Energizer who prods the group into action

Encourager who expresses warmth and solidarity as he/she praises, accepts, and encourages others

Harmonizer who seeks to ameliorate differences and relieve tensions

Expediter who interrupts those who monopolize discussion and tries to involve those who have not yet spoken

Follower who agrees with actions of the group and provides an audience for the more resourceful

Blocker who tends to disagree or revert to issues already resolved

Self-confessor who uses the meeting as a forum to express irrelevant personal feelings and beliefs

Dominator who is comfortable only when controlling the group

Help seeker who tries to get sympathy by admitting insecurity or confusion

Special interest pleader who acts out the part of a stereotype who inflicts biases on the group

Each team will reflect its own group dynamics, but there will usually be team members who play these parts to some degree. The following suggestions will help to enhance the use of planning periods.

1. **Accept your placement on the team as well as other members of the team.** Every middle school teacher may not have the opportunity to choose the other members of his/her teaching team. It is important, however, for a teacher to accept his/her position on a team in a professional way. It is also important to accept the other members of the team in a professional manner. Acceptance is the basis of good interpersonal

relationships among team members. Personality conflicts develop when acceptance and trust are not present.

2. **Promote exploration of the topic.** All team members should actively work to think through or explore all aspects of a topic. Questions that are open-ended help to facilitate exploration. Rather than simply voting to accept or reject a position or opinion of one team member, teachers should explore the pro's and con's of a given topic. Some time limits may need to be established and a procedure for determining consensus is needed; but this should not occur until all team members have contributed to a comprehensive exploration of the topic.

3. **Be honest in all communications.** Team members must learn to be honest with each other. Each team member must learn to be frank in answering questions and/or making comments. Teammates should know exactly what a colleague believes; they should not have to "guess" what the speaker really means. At times, team members are tempted to say what they think other team members or the school administration want them to say. Such a rationale will not foster open, honest communication.

4. **Use of the listening technique of reflection.** A good team member is a good listener. By being a good listener, one helps the speaker to clarify or be specific about thoughts. Reflection involves paraphrasing statements made by other team members to identify the feelings related to facts presented or statements made.

   The following statements are examples of reflection:

   "You are really not sure whether to teach that lesson tomorrow, right?"

   "You really disagree with us on that matter, but you are reluctant to say so."

   "The two of you seem to feel that we need to talk to the assistant principal about John. John's behavior really makes you angry!"

   In these examples, both content and affect are being reflected. Content is simply a summary of what is being discussed while affect describes the feelings or emotions associated with the facts. A good listener reflects both content and affect.

5. **Arrange the seating to promote good communication.** A circle type arrangement for seating is best. Team members are most likely to sit around a table which assures good eye contact. Guests should be seated in the same fashion as team members. Parents, for example, should be included in the circle. The team leader should not sit at a teacher's desk with others in front at student desks. Proper seating does much to facilitate equity and good communication.

6. **Non-verbal cues should be monitored.** Team members should be keenly aware of non-verbal messages sent out as they talk to each other or

to resource persons, parents, or others who attend team planning periods. Team members may be misled by relying on verbal statements without observing that which is communicated non-verbally.

The novice, on the other hand, should not be quick to evaluate non-verbal behavior. A particular gesture may mean many things depending on timing, content of the verbal discussion, or personality structure of the speaker. On the other hand, experienced, knowledgeable observers can interpret non-verbal cues in a meaningful way. Much can be learned about an individual from the non-spoken cues, and these non-verbal cues may contribute greatly to understanding that person and the message being delivered.

7. **Record decisions.** It is important to keep a written record of team decisions. A log may be requested by a school administrator; but, more importantly, it may be useful if a question arises in the future or if a team member wishes to be certain of a decision made. It may also be helpful to distribute written minutes to teachers on the team, especially if there are assignments to complete.

8. **Clarify the relationship of the team to the school and school system.** Even though the team may have some autonomy, it must still adhere to regulations of the school and school system. Team members must remember that there are rules and guidelines to follow; they may not do as they please on all matters. Planning is more effective when team members are fully aware of their privileges as well as their limitations.

CREATING AN AGENDA

The team leader should prepare an agenda for each team meeting. This can be posted on a chalkboard, bulletin board, or written for all team members and guests to see. Some typical agendas for interdisciplinary teams are:

TEAM 6A - September 15
1. Final adjustments to reading group assignments
2. School nurse to discuss several children with severe health problems
3. Initial discussion of plans for first PTA meeting
4. Evaluation of orientation program and specific follow-up activities in homeroom groups

TEAM 7B - October 20
1. Assessment of team effort to review functional reading skills
2. Referral of a student for special education services
3. Review of plans for a field trip to the Smithsonian in Washington, DC
4. Develop plan for "Following Directions" as the skill-of-the-week
5. Plan for teachers to preview museum display "Life in Ancient Egypt"

TEAM 8C - December 14
1. Correlate writing historical fiction activities between English and social studies
2. Evaluation of team effort to teach outlining skills in English, social studies, science, and mathematics
3. Plan for home base activity on conflict resolution
4. Plan for guidance counselor to discuss selection of courses for grade 9
5. Discussion of section change (within team) for Robert S.

Disciplinary or combination subject teams could have agendas such as:

Physical Education Team 6C - November 16
1. Evaluation of soccer unit recently completed
2. Discussion of problems in the locker room area
3. Plans to regroup students for the cross-country unit
4. Plans to record first quarter grades on the report card

Art/Music Team 7A - December 5
1. Plans for sectional rehearsals in band
2. Plans for a full chorus rehearsal
3. Special rehearsal schedule in preparation for winter concert
4. Guest speaker in art classes

Team members should determine the order of items on the agenda and time limits for each item. If an agenda item is not completed on one day, a time should be established to complete the discussion. Meetings should start and end on time. Conclusions should be put in writing and distributed to all appropriate persons.

USING SUBGROUPINGS OF THE TEAM

It is not always necessary for every item of team business to be completed during the designated team planning periods or by all team members. In fact, some items of business or action may be completed by a subcommittee of one or two members. It is important, however, for all team members to agree on the items that can be completed in subcommittee as contrasted with the items that require the presence and attention of all. Also, recommendations of sub-committees require approval of the full team. It is possible for subgroups to meet during the regularly scheduled planning periods. There should be a proper balance between items involving the full team and those that can be relegated to a subgroup so the team feeling or spirit is not lost.

Examples of items that can be accomplished by subgroups include:

Coordination of plans for field trips
Coordination of plans for assemblies and guest speakers
Scheduling of parent conferences
Coordination of home base program
Activities related to home base or skill-of-the-week programs
Writing team planning logs or summaries
Coordinating use of parent volunteers
Liaison with pupil services team conferences
Publication of weekly, biweekly, or monthly team newsletter

When subgroups take care of certain items, they should always report to the total team as well as for final approval or action. Subgroups utilize the strengths of team members and make the best use of time available.

INVOLVING PARENTS IN TEAM MEETINGS

Another valuable use of planning periods is to involve parents in groups or on an individual basis. These time periods can be used to orient parents to the teaming process, introduce parents to curricular materials, introduce skills or personal development activities, or have conferences about students' progress or problems. Many teams utilize these team planning periods to meet with the parents of a particular child about achievement and/or a problem.

Team members must be alert to the group dynamics of a parent conference. In many cases, this is the first real experience parents may have with middle school and teaming. If the conference goes well, the parents leave with positive feelings about both school and team. Parents know the developmental history of their child. Teachers know the effect of the peer group on that same individual. Thus, a collaborative partnership is needed to resolve problems at this stage of development. All participants should listen for feelings as well as content.

On the other hand, if the conference is not handled well, parents may become defensive and hostile. Teachers must be very sensitive to the interaction when parents meet with the team. The following suggestions are offered to help teams have positive contacts with parents:

1. Limit the amount of time a team devotes to parent conferences. If a team has three or four planning periods per week, one or two periods should be the maximum allocation for parent conferences.

2. Limit an individual parent conference to 15-20 minutes under normal circumstances.

3. Parents should be able to see an individual teacher without seeing the entire team. Only when appropriate should the entire team meet with parents.

4. The team leader should serve as moderator of the joint conferences.

5. The conference should begin on a positive, cheerful note. An effort should be made to establish positive rapport.

6. Teachers should be sincere, encouraging, and empathetic.

7. Each teacher present should make a brief statement about the child's performance. The statement should include some positive attribute. Examples and details should be offered as needed.

8. Parents should not be made to feel guilty about the performance of their children. They should have the opportunity to react to teachers' comments. A mutual dialogue should evolve. Questions should be "open-ended." Teachers should listen carefully to parents.

9. Teachers must present specific, constructive suggestions to help a child grow or improve.

10. Teachers should agree to keep parents informed of further developments.

11. The team leader, or another designated team member, should closely monitor the reaction of the parents. The team leader should intercede when verbal and/or non-verbal cues indicate.

12. Summary statements should be approved by all participants.

13. The team leader should provide closure by terminating the conference on a positive note and/or with an atmosphere of agreement on future goals. A commitment to follow-up is essential.

Conducting parent conferences is an important use of team planning periods, but they should not consume time needed to conduct other team business.

HANDLING DISCIPLINE PROBLEMS

Team meetings may also be used by teachers to resolve or at least discuss discipline problems. By developing a consistent team discipline code, focusing on the learning needs of each individual, and taking a positive approach, most problems will be reduced if not eliminated. Strategies available to the team include the following.

1. Invite the guidance counselor and administrator to join the team for a case study type of discussion

2. Invite parents to meet with the team to brief them about the problem and solicit their assistance before a situation is out of control

3. Utilize other pupil services specialists such as the school social worker or psychologist when necessary

4. Develop a behavior modification system utilizing the strengths of the team process

5. Determine if a change of section (within the team) would benefit the student

6. Bring the student into a team meeting to establish goals, priorities, or develop rapport if needed; be sensitive to how difficult this may be for the student

7. Issue awards or rewards on a weekly, monthly, or quarterly basis.

Generally, as the team works together, actions which ameliorate the difficulty will emerge.

INTERDISCIPLINARY UNITS

In addition to correlating content, skills, and personal development activities, thematic/interdisciplinary units may be created by teams of teachers as a centralized effort on the part of a faculty or school district. Thematic/interdisciplinary units are an excellent way for the early adolescent learner to see the wholeness of learning on a day by day basis as they experience teachers working together. Topics may include genealogy, baseball, animals, cooperation, consumer economics, safety, technology, or music.

With the leadership and inspiration of Judith Scheper and Lawrence Kimmel, the faculty of Hereford Middle School in Baltimore County (Maryland) organized a grade 8 interdisciplinary project to celebrate the achievement of students as they completed their experience in middle school. At the beginning of each school year, a planning committee was formed involving students, teachers, parents, and local businesses/ organizations.

Examples of interdisciplinary projects at Hereford Middle School include:

Space Commemoration Week. Inspired by the Teacher-In-Space project, and the *Challenger* Disaster, special activities included designing egg capsules for an egg drop, model airplane demonstrations, developing a time capsule, and a hot air balloon demonstration.

Waterworks. Focusing on water resources and the Chesapeake Bay, activities included: designing and racing model sailboats; stocking the Gunpowder River with fish; examining animals and artifacts of the region; visiting Baltimore's Inner Harbor for tours of the *Constellation*, the historic frigate; and sailing excursions.

Federal Fest. The activities spotlighted the Bicentennial of the *United States Constitution* and that time in history. This interdisciplinary unit recreated life during that important period.

2001: A Student Odyssey. Activities in this unit were designed to provide students a preview of what life may be like in the twenty-first century. Topics included computer applications in all curricular areas, robotics, lasers, telecommunication, biotechnology, synthesized music, careers of the future, and computer art.

In each of these thematic/interdisciplinary units, each subject area developed specialized enrichment lessons that provided hands-on opportunities to extend or apply the skills taught in that curricular area.

UTILIZING LOCAL OPTIONS

A major role of administrative/supervisory personnel in facilitating team success is to provide direction and leadership in establishing local options for teaching teams. Local options are those decisions that can be made by individual teaching teams either within guidelines created by the school system or in situations where guidelines have not been established.

The existence of local options may vary from district to district or school to school. It is essential that both administrative/ supervisory personnel and teachers understand what options exist. Generally, building principals are willing to let teams make decisions that will be compatible with school guidelines. Also, there is a relationship between the process by which curriculum is prescribed locally and opportunities for local options.

Some areas in which local options might exist include:

Correlating content. Was the curriculum written on an interdisciplinary basis with specific content items to be correlated identified? Or, was curriculum developed on a disciplinary basis and teachers encouraged to identify opportunities for correlation?

Selecting the skill-of-the-week. Is there a chronological guide listing the skill-of-the-week for each week of the year at each grade level or are teams free to identify the skills appropriate for students?

Selecting topics for home base activities. Is there a list of home base units to be taught each week at each grade level or are teachers free to choose activities they believe students need?

Determining the number of periods per week for meeting with parents. A school or school system may determine the number of team planning periods that can be used for parent conferences or each team may make its own decision as to how many planning periods may be made available for conferences and how many should be reserved for other team business.

Flexible scheduling. What guidelines exist in the area of flexible scheduling? Are all decisions about scheduling made by the principal or are teams free to make their own decisions?

Regrouping students for instruction. Are teams of teachers able to make all decisions about regrouping independently or must all decisions about re-grouping have approval from a member of the administrative/supervisory staff?

Field trips. Are certain field trips prescribed for students in grades 6, 7, and/or 8? Or, are teachers able to make decisions about field trips according to the curriculum or specific student needs? Are some field trips required and others optional? To what extent are these field trips an opportunity for interdisciplinary instruction?

Assemblies. Assemblies are routinely scheduled for the school or grade on topics of interest for early adolescents. Additionally, assemblies can be arranged by teams, clusters, or houses on a local option basis. This may help to build team spirit and identify as well as permit in-depth exploration of specific topics of interest.

Community service. As the unique personality of a team emerges, community service activities can be organized on a local option basis. One team can work with the elderly while another helps to beautify the neighborhood. Sections within teams can have their own community service projects as the team orchestrates a total effort for involvement.

This list is not exhaustive; it is merely a sampling of topics. Administrative/supervisory personnel play a key role in determining which items can be accomplished on a local option basis and in helping teachers to take advantage of these opportunities. Once these local options are established, administrative/supervisory personnel can monitor the extent to which teachers utilize them and the outcomes of these efforts.

SUMMARY

Strategies for the effective use of planning periods were presented as teachers must see the relationship between planning periods and the instructional program. Group dynamics play a key role in the success of the teaming relationship. An agenda should be developed for each team meeting. Sub-groupings of the team can meet for certain purposes. Parents can participate in team meetings, and team planning periods can be used to resolve discipline problems. Teachers should be aware of and utilize the local options available to them in planning thematic/interdisciplinary units.

Activity:

1. How many team planning periods exist in our schedule?

2. What are our primary responsibilities as a teaching team?

3. If time permits, what other responsibilities might we assume?

4. How can we monitor the extent to which we implement the eight recommendations for facilitating group dynamics?

5. Do we have an agenda for each meeting? How is it formulated?

6. When do we utilize subgroupings of the team? How successful is this approach for us?

7. How effective are conferences with parents? Do parents leave pleased with the opportunity to meet with the team members?

8. Does the team provide a good forum to resolve discipline problems?

9. How effective is our utilization of the planning periods? What changes might we make?

10. What opportunities exist for interdisciplinary units?

11. What are our local options? How can we find out if we have a local option in a given situation?

9

Using Flexible
Scheduling Techniques

A key to the success of the teaming process is the extent to which teachers use flexible scheduling techniques. Traditionally, the schedule in junior and senior high schools is characterized by sameness. The order of the classes is the same; the time duration for each of the classes is the same. This condition is the result of the requirements of Carnegie units and tradition. In high schools, principals must certify that a student attended each class for fifty minutes per day as part of the college admissions process. Because ninth graders accumulate credits toward graduation from high school, the structure of the high school affected the middle level school. Junior high teachers were unable to shorten or lengthen a class period, change the number of periods in a given day, change the order of the periods within the day, or do other special innovative activities because each class had to be fifty minutes in accordance with Carnegie units.

In the middle school, such rigidity is not necessary. Even if ninth graders are assigned to the middle level school, the concept of flexibility can be implemented in the other grades. Flexibility is a response to rapid physical growth, short attention span, fatigue, and the fact that students are at different stages of development. Without the impact of Carnegie units, middle school teachers can plan the instructional program according to student needs.

WHAT IS FLEXIBLE SCHEDULING?

Flexible scheduling suggests that the order of each day need not be the same. Group size, the order of the periods, and the length of each period can vary. Flexible scheduling is not a concept that can be mandated by the school administration. Rather, once the provisions for flexible scheduling are put into place, it is up to the teachers to take advantage of opportunities to be flexible in planning daily, weekly, or monthly schedules.

Flexible scheduling is a way of responding to developmental needs of early adolescents. As students go through various physical and mental changes, attention span varies. Some lessons should be 30 or 35 minutes in length; other lessons, if planned properly, can be 60-65 minutes.

A student should not always have algebra seventh period of the day. If a student has physical education each day of the week, it would be helpful to have the class in the morning on some days and the afternoon on other days.

Variety is important for teachers and students. Although flexible scheduling requires many decisions by teachers about student needs, content, and even teaching strategies, the approach should be viewed in light of the benefits for students.

Flexible scheduling should also be viewed as an excellent way to achieve the structure needed for the total team program. In order to have a reading program, a home base or teacher/advisory program, special assemblies, a strong skills program, and other activities, it is necessary for the team to make some decisions about how time will be allotted for those various supplements to the curriculum.

For example, a sixth grade interdisciplinary team of four teachers may wish to provide time for spelling and handwriting activities as a total team experience rather than restrict it to the domain of the language arts teacher. These teachers would then work together to plan the program, identify time allocations for these activities, and evaluate the effectiveness of this approach. In this example, teachers must make decisions about how the total time frame will be used to present the composite program that best meets the needs of students.

Finally, flexible scheduling is an excellent way for teachers to develop the team relationships described in previous sections. The discussions about schedule enable teachers to really get to know each other, work through expectations, resolve differences, and work toward team goals. Rather than discussing some superficial topic, teams can approach items mandating flexible scheduling in a way that truly facilitates team building.

Flexible scheduling is a concept, a point-of-view, and a basis for teachers to work together to achieve a common goal — the best possible learning experience for pupils. In order to achieve flexibility, there must be a block-of-time schedule and teachers who are willing to utilize flexible or modular strategies. This chapter will introduce techniques for utilizing the block-of-time, creating rotating schedules, designing modular subdivisions of time, and building alternate day rotations.

BLOCK-OF-TIME SCHEDULING

Block-of-time scheduling permits two or more teachers of two or more subjects to teach those classes during the same block-of-time. For example, an English, social studies, mathematics, and science teacher in grade 7 have the same four classes for periods 1-4 each day. These teachers have, in essence, a total of 200 minutes of instruction for the 110 pupils on the team. They have common planning periods outside the block during which they can plan cooperatively.

A second example might be an art and music teacher who have the same 54 students first period on Monday, second period on Tuesday and Wednesday, and sixth period on Thursday and Friday. The teachers can regroup or subdivide the pupils however they choose. If all pupils are singing in the chorus, the chorus teacher could form a soprano group and an alto group. Sopranos would be in music and art together. On some days, all 54 pupils could be in chorus; on other days, all 54 pupils could see a film or hear a guest speaker in art. The responsibility for sub-dividing the pupils rests with the two teachers involved. No other portion of the schedule is affected once the blocks are set.

Block-of-time scheduling is also a factor in single-subject teams. Two mathematics teachers may share fifty-five pupils for Algebra I period 3 each day. The same students must be scheduled with the same teachers each day to permit the regrouping of pupils based on their achievement.

There is a difference between interdisciplinary team organization and block-of-time. To be an interdisciplinary team, the three, four or five teachers do not have to be scheduled at the same time. Although it is most advisable, it is not mandatory. Block-of-time requires that the teachers involved are, in fact, teaching at the same times. Ideally, all interdisciplinary teams (as well as core/combination and disciplinary teams) would be on a block-of-time basis.

ROTATING SCHEDULES

One of the benefits of the block-of-time approach is the option of a rotating schedule. Since there are four teaching sections, there can be four options for the rotations or sequences of the classes through the various subjects of the interdisciplinary team. In this way, each section can experience each of the options for an equal amount of time during the school year. If there are advantages and/or disadvantages of any options, teaching sections have equal opportunity for both advantages and disadvantages. Rotations can be biweekly, monthly, or quarterly.

The following examples will demonstrate the steps in creating a rotating schedule. For each period that the students are in the interdisciplinary team, each section attends one subject. For example, the schedule for second period on Wednesday could be:

WEDNESDAY

PERIOD	SECTION	SUBJECT
2	1	Science
	2	Mathematics
	3	Social Studies
	4	English

The concept of rotation is then expanded to the entire day as follows.

WEDNESDAY

2	1	Science
	2	Mathematics
	3	Social Studies
	4	English

3	1	English
	2	Science
	3	Mathematics
	4	Social Studies

LUNCH

4	1	Social Studies
	2	English
	3	Science
	4	Mathematics

5	1	Mathematics
	2	Social Studies
	3	English
	4	Science

This concept is then expanded for the entire week as demonstrated in these schedules.

SECTION #1

Period	Mon.	Tues.	Wed.	Thurs.	Fri.
1					
2	English	English	English	English	
3	Soc.Studies	Soc.Studies	Soc.Studies	Soc.Studies	English
4	Math		Science		Soc.Studies
5	Science	Math	Math	Math	Math
6		Science		Science	Science
7					

SECTION #2

Period	Mon.	Tues.	Wed.	Thurs.	Fri.
1					
2	Soc.Studies	Soc.Studies	Soc.Studies	Soc.Studies	
3	Math	Math	Math	Math	Soc.Studies
4	Science		Science		Math
5	English	Science	English	Science	Science
6		English		English	English
7					

SECTION #3

Period	Mon.	Tues.	Wed.	Thurs.	Fri.
1					
2	Math	Math	Math	Math	
3	Science	Science	Science	Science	Math
4	English		Soc.Studies		Science
5	Soc.Studies	English	English	English	English
6		Soc.Studies		Soc.Studies	Soc.Studies
7					

SECTION #4

Period	Mon.	Tues.	Wed.	Thurs.	Fri.
1					
2	Science	Science	Science	Science	
3	English	English	English	English	Science
4	Soc.Studies		Math		English
5	Math	Soc.Studies	Soc.Studies	Soc.Studies	Soc.Studies
6		Math		Math	Math
7					

Activity:

1. What is the commitment of our school and/or team to the concept of flexible scheduling?

2. To what extent does the administration of the school encourage the use of flexible scheduling?

3. What is our accountability as we utilize flexible scheduling?

4. Have the persons who built the master schedule provided blocks-of-time for our team?

5. To what extent do we want to utilize block-of-time opportunities that exist in our schedule?

6. How effectively do we communicate (as a team) our wishes to utilize the block-of-time opportunities that exist?

7. How will we evaluate our use of block-of-time?

8. What rotations are possible for our team?

9. Who will take the initiative in designing the rotations?

MODULAR SUBDIVISIONS OF TIME

When the block-of-time concept has been utilized in constructing the master schedule, opportunities for modular subdivisions of time exist. A module refers to an amount of time other than the usual period. Modules can be 10, 15, 20, 25, 30, 35, or 40 minutes. Smaller modules suggest greater flexibility. A modular approach can be used to divide blocks-of-time for various activities. An eighth grade team may wish to use a flexible/modular schedule to implement a home base program as well as a free reading activity.

Traditional Grade 8
8:30 - 8:40 - Homeroom
8:40 - 9:30 - Period 1 - Algebra I
9:30 - 10:20 - Period 2 - English
10:20 - 11:10 - Period 3 - Art
11:10 - 12:00 - Period 4 - Physical Education
12:00 - 12:30 - LUNCH
12:30 - 1:20 - Period 5 - French I
1:20 - 2:10 - Period 6 - Social Studies
2:10 - 3:00 - Period 7 - Science

Flexible/Modular Approach Grade 8
8:30 - 8:50 - Homeroom and Home base Activities
8:50 - 9:35 - Period 1 - Algebra I
9:35 - 10:20 - Period 2 - English
10:20 - 11:10 - Period 3 - Art
11:10 - 12:00 - Period 4 - Physical Education
12:00 - 12:30 - LUNCH
12:30 - 1:00 - Reading Activity
1:00 - 1:40 - Period 5 - French I
1:40 - 2:20 - Period 6 - Social Studies
2:20 - 3:00 - Period 7 - Science

In grade 6, for example, the teachers may choose to divide the 150 minute block-of-time to find time for intensive spelling and handwriting instruction in addition to the regular program of studies.

12:00 - 12:30 - LUNCH
12:30 - 1:00 - Spelling, Handwriting Activities
1:00 - 1:40 - Period 5
1:40 - 2:20 - Period 6
2:20 - 3:00 - Period 7

A seventh grade team could create a 15 or 20 minute module in which to introduce the skill-of-the-week and still allow pupils to see all their teachers that day.

When modular subdivisions of time are utilized, frequency and duration of class meetings are determined by teachers. These decisions should be based upon instructional tasks and needs of students. All courses need not meet every day. The time allocated for a given activity depends on the nature of that activity. Teams of teachers are encouraged to think of all possible modular subdivisions of time as they plan a variety of activities to meet the learning needs of students.

In the example below, the goal of the teaching team was to provide an opportunity for students to attend all four classes during a two period block-of-time prior to lunch. This plan could be utilized on a day when the students would only be in school until noon or if a special event were to be scheduled in the afternoon.

Time	Wednesday
9:30	Create
	Four
	25 Minute
11:10	Modules

A variation of the above schedule would be when a three-member team needed to subdivide the 100 minutes into three periods.

Situations may arise when members of the team would like to create a 75 minute module followed by a 25 minute module. This scheme could be utilized when the science teacher planned a laboratory lesson, when any teachers of the team planned a lesson to introduce a new unit of study, or when one or more teachers scheduled an independent study program. This model is for a lesson that consists of activities that would sustain the interest of students for 75 minutes or would require more time to be completed.

This concept of modular subdivision of time can be extended to the entire day or to the amount of time the teachers are responsible for the students on that team. For example, the team of teachers may wish to plan a special orientation for students on the first day of school. The schedule below will provide teachers an opportunity to do an orientation session in large groups, see each section for 40 minutes, and then have a follow-up activity for the last 30 minutes that the students are assigned to the team. On this schedule, students are away from the team until 9:30 a.m. and after 2:10 p.m.

Time	Wednesday	
9:30 to 10:30	ORIENTATION SESSION	
	SECTION/SUBJECT	
10:30 to 11:10	1	Mathematics
	2	Social Studies
	3	English
	4	Science
11:10 to 11:40	LUNCH	
	SECTION/SUBJECT	
11:40 to 12:20	1	Social Studies
	2	English
	3	Science
	4	Mathematics
12:20 to 1:00	1	Science
	2	Mathematics
	3	Social Studies
	4	English
1:00 to 1:40	1	English
	2	Science
	3	Mathematics
	4	Social Studies
1:40 to 2:10	FOLLOW-UP ACTIVITY	

ALTERNATE DAY ROTATIONS

The final application of flexible scheduling is alternate day rotations. This approach provides an opportunity for disciplinary and core/combination teams to become flexible. An example of an alternate day rotation is when an art teacher and a music teacher are scheduled on a parallel, block-of-time basis with the same 50 students for these courses. On day one, half of the students are in each course; on day two, students attend the other course. Classes meet every other day or five times within two weeks.

Alternate day rotations permit teachers to combine classes when appropriate and regroup students according to needs of students and parameters of the program. More specifically, all of the students involved in this parallel could be chorus students. Thus, the music teacher could subgroup the students according to soprano, alto, or tenor. As a student's voice might change as a function of physical development, regrouping could occur.

Typical alternate day rotations include:

1.   Physical Education/General Music
2.   Physical Education/Chorus
3.   Foreign Language/Computers
4.   Art/Computers
5.   Electives/Physical Education
6.   Woodwind Instruments/Art
7.   Brass Instruments/Art
8.   Percussion Instruments/Art
9.   Stringed Instruments/Art

Other courses could be included in these alternate day rotations.

Alternate day rotations provide an opportunity for regrouping students as well as having the subjects rotate on a daily, weekly, monthly, or quarterly basis. For example, as the chorus prepares for a concert, the teacher might want all students for the week prior to the concert so the choral presentation can be refined. If the school system offers electives on a quarterly basis, the alternate day rotation model can be utilized.

SUMMARY

Flexible scheduling techniques permit a team of teachers to develop a comprehensive curriculum that responds to the particular needs of their pupils. Obviously, needs vary from team to team. Block-of-time scheduling is needed to facilitate modular subdivisions. As teachers utilize flexible scheduling techniques, pupils benefit.

Activity:

1. What opportunities for modular scheduling exist within our team schedule?

2. How can we assess the attention span limitations of our pupils?

3. What are some of the special needs of our students that can best be met by using a modular approach?

4. What alternate day rotations exist in our schedule? How can we utilize these opportunities to improve our delivery of instruction?

5. How will we inform students of these changes in the schedule?

6. How will we evaluate the effectiveness of our modular/flexible scheduling strategies?

10
Grouping and Regrouping
Pupils for Instruction

The team process should provide opportunities to group and regroup students for a variety of educational purposes. In many schools, 25-30 students are known as a class and, for the most part, remain together as a group for the six or seven periods of the day. In other schools, students are "individually scheduled" so that a student could conceivably be in six or seven different groupings with as many as 150-200 different pupils each day and not really be able to make friends with or psychologically identify with more than a few students. The effective middle school organizational plan should be somewhere between these extremes.

In the middle school, interdisciplinary teams can be created for 100-140 pupils, disciplinary teams can be formed for 50-140 pupils in a single subject, and core/combination subject teams can be designed for 50-85 pupils for a block of two or three subjects. In each of these situations, pupils can be grouped initially and then subsequently regrouped. The concept of flexible grouping of students is another way middle schools can respond to ever-changing developmental needs of early adolescents.

EXAMPLES OF TEAM ORGANIZATION OR SETTINGS

Middle schools organize students for instructional purposes as part of the overall scheduling process. It is essential that teachers are aware of the organization and implications of the scheduling process for the day-to-day teaching of students. Several organizational options are possible.

Interdisciplinary. A middle school with interdisciplinary teams and some ability grouping may organize four or five classes per grade level into teams. The plan could be like the examples below.

92

GRADE 7

Sections of Team 7A	Sections of Team 7B
#1 - Standard	#1 - Gifted and Talented
#2 - Standard	#2 - Standard
#3 - Standard	#3 - Standard
#4 - Below Grade Level	#4 - Standard

In this example, approximately 110 pupils could be assigned to Team 7A and another 110 pupils assigned to Team 7B. There would be an English, social studies, mathematics, and science teacher on each of the teams. Pupils could be assigned to one of the four teaching sections of each of the teams by the administration, guidance counselor, and/or classroom teachers. This is an example of initial grouping of students within the interdisciplinary team model.

Pupils do not need to remain in these original groupings for the entire year. Perhaps a pupil experienced a major growth spurt during the summer, profited greatly from a remedial reading program, or was truly motivated to achieve by the present team of teachers. Teachers can change a student's section within the team or even create an individualized schedule for a student who should be in a Gifted and Talented section for mathematics and science but standard section for social studies and English.

Cross-team regrouping is also possible. A student could be enrolled in two Gifted and Talented courses on Team 7B and two standard courses on Team 7A. A student could be enrolled in two below grade level classes on Team 7A and two standard classes on Team 7B. A handicapped student could participate in two standard classes on 7B and two special education courses. Adjustments to the grouping arrangements are an on-going responsibility of the teachers on the interdisciplinary team.

Disciplinary. A school may assign a block of 100 pupils to physical education with the same four physical education teachers at the same time. All of the pupils on interdisciplinary team 7A could go to physical education at the same time. Each pupil could then be assigned to one of the four physical education teachers for home base purposes — taking roll, recording and posting grades, counseling — but actually be in a different group (with a different teacher) for various units of instruction.

Pupils could be assigned to an instructional group according to level of skill, prior experience, or interests. In a gymnastics unit, for example, pupils could be grouped by performance level. At other times, pupils could select archery, badminton, volleyball, or soccer. Pupils could rotate among the teachers on a round-robin basis. By the end of the school year, each of the four physical education teachers would know each of the pupils; and the students will have completed a comprehensive physical education program geared to the varied interests, skills, and needs of individuals within the group.

A second example of a single subject team might be reading in grade 6. Two teachers could be paired for 48 students or two sections. One might teach language arts and social studies to both sections while the other specializes in mathematics and science for both sections. But, the two teachers teach reading at the same time for the 48 students. In fact, the two sixth grade teachers could be joined by the school's reading specialist one period every day to provide reading instruction for the 48 students in three groups.

The three professionals might choose to group these pupils for reading accordingly:

Reading Teacher
Group #1 - Remedial Group - 3rd & 4th grade levels - 8 pupils

Teacher A (Language Arts/Social Studies)
Group #2 - 5-2 Basal - 10 students
Group #3 - 6-1 Basal - 10 students

Teacher B (Math/Science)
Group #4 - 6-2 Basal - 10 students
Group #5 - 7-1 and above - 10 students

These three staff members are operating their own disciplinary team as an independent variable. They could regroup pupils at any time according to the growth and development of each student. Grouping in reading does not affect grouping for any other part of the instructional program.

A third example of a disciplinary team in the middle school could be Algebra I in grade 8. Two mathematics teachers could be responsible for 50 students. They could begin the school year with a diagnostic test and group the students into two groups of 25 for a review of integers, associative law, commutative law, rational numbers, or any other topic in Mathematics 7 that would be important in the first unit of Algebra I.

At this point, the teachers could form two groups and teach the first unit concurrently. At the end of the first unit, they would give the same unit test. After the test was scored, pupils who did well (in either section) could be given enrichment work by one teacher while the other teacher could offer remedial work and eventually retest pupils in either group who did poorly on the test. The teachers could then begin to teach Unit II with all pupils closer to the same level of cognition. This process could be repeated throughout the year. Grouping could be a function of cumulative achievement.

Core/combination subject team. A chorus teacher and art teacher could be scheduled on a parallel basis with 50 students for the two subjects. They could meet and decide to have the chorus teacher divide the students into two groups based on soprano/alto, ability to read music, or some other basis. With the cooperation of the art teacher, the chorus teacher could regroup individual students between the two sections during the course of the school year based on performance factors in chorus.

Team organizations not mutually exclusive. It is important to remember that the three team organizational patterns are not mutually exclusive. A seventh grader could be on an interdisciplinary team for English, social studies, mathematics, and science; a disciplinary team for physical education; a core/combination team for art and music; and a second core/combination team for technology education, home economics, and foreign language. Grouping decisions in each of the team settings are independent of others; therefore, a student can be grouped and regrouped based on needs and performance factors in each of these settings. The common bond would be the student grouping called Team 7A. Generally, the interdisciplinary subject teachers are the advisory group that coordinates the entire process.

WHAT ARE WE TRYING TO ACCOMPLISH BY GROUPING AND REGROUPING?

The team organization in the middle school facilitates grouping and regrouping students. These regrouping practices should help to bring about the optimum learning environment for the student within an environment that has the structure and security needed for early adolescent learners.

Focusing on needs of students. Each team — interdisciplinary, disciplinary, or core/combination — should focus on needs of students. Each team needs common planning time as part of the work day to focus on students within that portion of the instructional program. Whether a team is made up of 50, 80, or 120 students, the teachers on that team have the obligation to view each student as an individual. Each student is going through a series of developmental changes at his or her own rate; no one student is exactly like another.

Teachers must resist the temptation to look at or talk about one class or another class. They need to recognize that classes are made up of individuals; and they must look at the motivation, readiness, home background, reading scores, mathematics scores, and interests of each individual. The team becomes the vehicle to respond to such needs. At times, it becomes necessary to adjust the instructional program or instructional level of an individual student; and the grouping/regrouping process is one way a team shows its concern for individuals.

Enhancing the self-concept. A pupil needs variety during the course of the day and should not be with the same 25-30 students for all seven periods. This is especially true if a child is a slow learner or is learning disabled. These youngsters need opportunities to interact with others the same age in experiences where the disability or limitation will not restrict the opportunity to learn. Courses such as art, music, physical education, technology education, and home economics should present opportunities to truly reach all pupils in heterogeneous situations.

By the same token, Gifted and Talented students need opportunities to mix with other students. By placing G & T pupils into interdisciplinary teams that are heterogeneous in their total composition, these students will have chances to meet and work with other students. They need the opportunity to be with others as much as the slow learners.

The middle school experience should help, not hinder, the development of a positive self-concept. By grouping and regrouping students, the student has varied opportunities to develop a positive view of self. With the additional support of counseling and home base activities, the total curriculum can provide ample positive experiences.

ROLE OF THE COUNSELOR AND PUPIL DATA SYSTEMS

Guidance counselors play a key role in grouping students. Although counselors usually work closely with administrators and classroom teachers in developing lists for the initial grouping of students, it is even more important for counselors to work with the various teams during the course of the school year to identify opportunities for regrouping.

Counselors have access to all data needed to monitor student development during the early adolescent years. Types of data needed to help teachers understand students and provide the necessary levels of instruction include:

1. Record of achievement in previous grades

2. Performance on standardized achievement tests

3. Performance on standardized tests of scholastic aptitude or mental ability

4. Performance on interest inventories or career preference instruments

5. Performance on individually administered personality or educational assessment measures

6. Performance on functional reading/mathematics/writing tests

7. Anecdotal reports in the cumulative folder

8. Rating scales completed in prior years

9. Questionnaire surveys completed by the student

10. Autobiographies, case studies

11. Records of home visits or social histories

12. Interview record of the counselor

Data have limitations, and counselors need to help place data elements in proper perspective. By attending team planning periods on a regular basis, counselors can help teachers make decisions about the regrouping of youngsters to achieve the best learning environment.

REGROUPING FOR SPECIAL ACTIVITIES

In addition to regrouping pupils from one teaching situation to another for English, physical education, algebra, or chorus, the opportunity exists to regroup students for special activities such as functional reading, spelling, handwriting, skills lab, or home base.

1. **Reading.** Middle schools use varied approached for teaching reading. A basal reading program may exist in grade six with reading taught through the various content areas and/or by special regrouping within interdisciplinary teams.

    One approach to teaching functional reading skills could involve all four or five teachers of the interdisciplinary team in grade 6 or 7. Five domains exist in the area of functional reading: following directions, locating information from reference sources, gaining information from the main idea, gaining information using details, and understanding forms.

    Each of the teachers could develop a packet of materials or a mini-unit on one domain; pupils would rotate on a round-robin basis several modules per week over a period of weeks to attend all five programs. Pupils could be grouped according to performance on a preassessment device or in homogeneous or heterogeneous groups. Utilizing an alternative arrangement is wise for such an activity.

    At the eighth grade level, pupils reading below grade level might take a reading skills course in conjunction with an English course. This course could be team taught by the reading teacher and the English teacher. On certain days, both teachers would be available to teach these students. Pupils could be regrouped according to specific aspects of the program such as reading for main ideas, use of context clues or sequencing skills. Pupils could be regrouped according to strengths and weaknesses on specific skills during the course of the school year.

2. **Spelling/handwriting.** In middle schools where sixth grade pupils are in four teacher teams, there is often not an opportunity for the or language arts teacher to implement a specific program for spelling

and/or handwriting; on the other hand, self-contained elementary school teachers can have spelling and handwriting activities on a regular basis.

By using modular scheduling techniques, all of the teachers on the team could allocate some time each week for spelling and handwriting activities. Pupils could be regrouped according to levels of spelling proficiency for spelling and handwriting activities. Different sources for words could be used with different groups. Pupils would benefit from having their science teacher, for example, teaching spelling and handwriting.

3. **Skills lab.** Using modular scheduling, a team of teachers could work together to present a skills lab program. Skills included might be writing a science laboratory report, reading for details, improving listening skills, note-taking skills, or distinguishing between fact and opinion.

   These skills could be presented on an interdisciplinary basis; pupils could be assigned on a homogeneous or heterogeneous basis, depending on the preference of the teachers and/or needs of students. By involving other staff members, pupils could be scheduled in groups of 15-20 for the skills laboratory program.

4. **Home base or teacher/advisory.** Another opportunity for re-grouping pupils for special activities involves the home base or teacher/advisory program. Each homeroom teacher (usually an interdisciplinary team teacher) would have that group as advisees, and each could present the same home base activity each time. Another option is, however, for teachers to become "specialists" in an aspect of the home base curriculum such as resolving conflict, decision-making, communication skills, or helping the handicapped. By having the teachers "specialize," pupils could be regrouped for these sessions on a round-robin basis.

5. **Assemblies and other large group situations.** A final example of regrouping for special activities would be to have assemblies or large group presentations for two, three, four, or all five sections within a team. A guest speaker, panel discussion, or thematic unit culminating activity could be presented. After a large group activity, follow-up discussions might be arranged involving small groups representing the various teaching sections of the team.

COMMUNICATIONS WITH PARENTS AND STUDENTS

Parents as well as students must understand the process of grouping and re-grouping for instruction. At an open-house before school starts or at the first PTA meeting in September, teachers should explain how pupils are grouped into teams and teaching sections within teams. Parents should be familiar with grouping procedures used in each of their child's courses.

Also, parents should be aware of the team's philosophy of regrouping for special activities. This can be explained in a team newsletter distributed early in the school year. Parents who understand the reason will support changes in routine.

Students must also understand the team's philosophy of grouping and regrouping. As changes are made, the reasons should be reiterated. Changes should be received by students in a positive way, not as a threat to their security or self-concept. Schedules of special activities such as reading, spelling, or home base should be posted on bulletin boards and announced by teachers. Pupils will soon recognize these changes and adjustments as the norm, not the exception.

At the end of the school year, parents and students could participate in an evaluation of the team's efforts in the area of grouping and regrouping. A simple instrument could be designed to assess the cognitive and affective reaction to philosophy and practices. The results could be correlated with achievement growth as well as attitude surveys created by the team or guidance counselor. The team could then measure the extent to which the grouping practices contributed to the team's success.

SUMMARY

Grouping and regrouping for instructional purposes is a key element of the team process in the middle school. Once teachers understand the structure of the master schedule, they are in a position to utilize grouping and regrouping strategies to meet unique needs of each student.

Team planning sessions should be devoted to exploring opportunities for grouping and regrouping. As teachers implement the curriculum and strive to meet the needs of students, there could be almost no end to the opportunities for grouping and regrouping students in grades 6, 7, and 8.

Activity:

1. What opportunities exist in the master schedule for interdisciplinary teaching?

2. What opportunities exist in the master schedule for disciplinary team teaching?

3. What opportunities exist in the master schedule for core/combination subject teams?

4. How will pupils initially be grouped in each of these team situations?

5. What are the school's guidelines on regrouping pupils for instructional purposes within a given team?

6. How will our team handle regrouping pupils?

7. How will parents and students be informed of regrouping decisions?

8. How will our team evaluate its efforts to group and regroup pupils for instructional purposes?

9. How will pupils be grouped and regrouped for special activities on our team?

11

Resolving Conflicts
Among Team Members

Conflicts will occur among team members. It is inevitable because the team approach to instruction calls for teachers to work with one another in situations that call for extensive communication, interaction, and cooperation. Most teachers now working in teams had no preparation for teaming. Now as they start working in clusters, conflicts will arise. Differences need to be resolved, and decisions should be collaborative. Resolving conflict should be viewed as positive, developmental, and a productive means to an end. To achieve full ownership of the situation, all involved should contribute to the resolution.

In this chapter, case studies are presented to illustrate the types of conflicts that may occur and how these conflicts can be resolved. Following the statement of the problem or case study, questions are presented to guide further discussion of these situations. Instead of specific answers to these questions, each scenario will include key factors to be considered in helping the group resolve the conflict or potential conflict in a positive way.

Case Study #1

A science teacher on a seventh grade team was viewed by the others as an individualist, not a team player. The teacher was not in favor of team field trips. Instead, the teacher only wanted to take one section at a time on a trip related to the science curriculum. Further, this teacher did not teach or try to reinforce the skill-of-the-week program. Although the teacher was present during team planning periods, there were no indicators in the classroom or in lesson plans of any effort to teach, extend, or reinforce the skills identified. On many occasions, this teacher gave lengthy "speeches" to other members of the team on how to teach seventh grade students. Because the teacher did not support the team in other ways, team members were not responsive to the suggestions and clearly resisted adopting the philosophy presented.

Guide Questions

1. Is there a pattern to the actions of this teacher? If so, what is that pattern?

2. What is this teacher trying to say to the other members of the team?

3. Thus far, how have the other members of the team received the message?

4. What specific strategies might be utilized to resolve this conflict?

In answering these questions, consider the difficulty the teacher may be experiencing in making the transition from junior high to middle school. Consider also whether the symptoms described may be part of a larger issue rather than simply opposition to the teaming process. In resolving the problem, try to help this teacher, but do not let the team process be subordinated to the needs of this individual teacher.

Case Study #2

In the year of transition, a number of teachers were given the opportunity to transfer to high schools. In this way, the school district was helping to facilitate the success of the ninth grade program as well as the success of the middle school program. The mathematics teacher assigned to one of the grade 8 teams wanted to be at the high school but lacked the seniority to obtain that position. As a result, this teacher was angry. At team meetings, he expressed that anger and indicated that "junior high school students do not want to learn" and that "junior high school students do not appreciate his efforts." Although this teacher attended every team meeting, the teacher did not participate in team discussions.

Guide Questions

1. How can this teacher be helped to accept the assignment in middle school?

2. Specifically, how can some of this anger be sublimated into more positive directions?

3. What staff development activities might enable this person to alter the attitude demonstrated?

In answering these questions, consider the possible need for more information about the developmental nature of middle school students, the emphasis on mathematics in the training of that teacher, and the fear of the unknown. Many of these factors may be impacting upon this individual who may or may not respond to other team members reaching out to help. Part of the problem may be the misperception of this individual about the nature of the learning process.

Case Study #3

As a member of a three-person sixth grade interdisciplinary team, one of the teachers emerges as a domineering personality who wants to be in total control of the team process. In an effort to accomplish this goal, the teacher volunteers to do all of the team tasks. Additionally, this person is the first to speak on topics for discussion and reacts vehemently to dissenting thoughts. In most cases, the individual is inflexible in resolving conflicts.

Guide Questions

1. What might be the underlying reasons for the actions of this individual?

2. To what extent have other team members permitted this to occur?

3. What strategies could be suggested to the other two teachers to minimize the effect of this domineering personality?

4. If all else fails, what actions should the other team members take?

In answering these questions, consider the personality needs of the domineering teacher. In many ways these actions may be compensatory for attention or recognition not received elsewhere. It is also possible that this individual wants very much to be promoted to an administrative position and sees the team process as a means to that end. It is the responsibility of other team members to guarantee that final decisions are in the best educational interests of students.

Case Study #4

One of the four physical education teachers assigned to a single subject team is always late for meetings. After arriving, the teacher does not participate in discussions. Instead, the teacher grades papers or prepares rosters for intramural games. When invited to participate in discussions, this individual declines.

Guide Questions

1. What are some reasons that this person chooses not to participate in the team process?

2. What strategies could be utilized to increase the involvement of this teacher?

In answering these questions, consider the possibility that this teacher is uncomfortable sharing teaching techniques with others. For many years, this teacher may have worked in a traditional setting on an independent basis. This teacher may feel inferior to one or more members of the team and uses avoidance to shield those feelings. The objectives are to enhance communication and protect the self-concept of all team members.

Case Study #5

Because of a reorganization of teaching teams, two teachers who worked together previously find themselves teamed with persons new to the building. Rather than trying to build a strong unity among the four teachers, the two who worked together previously became a clique within the team. Through their statements and actions, it becomes apparent that they were more interested in their ideas and needs as opposed to the needs of the entire team or the ideas of others.

Guide Questions

1. What team building activities could be used to help create a bond among the four teachers in this situation?

2. How could the two novice teachers utilize team planning meetings to discuss their exclusion from the clique?

3. What opportunities could be created for each of the veteran teachers to work with each new teacher on a specific team responsibility?

4. How could the evaluation process be utilized to identify or ameliorate this problem?

5. At the end of the school year, how might the building administrator approach the decision to keep this team intact for the next year?

In answering these questions, consider the security needs of the returning teachers as well as the apparent insecurity of the newly assigned teachers. Team building activities may or may not solve the problem. In reality, the insecurity of the two veteran teachers may be greater than the insecurity of the new teachers. A key to success in this case is pairing veteran and novice teachers on specific tasks. A structured evaluation process at the end of the first semester would also help.

Case Study #6

The art teacher talked to the principal about being excluded from the planning process. On the one hand, the art teacher complained about "babysitting" students so the interdisciplinary team teachers could have a meeting. On the other hand, in response to some questions from the principal, the art teacher expressed a real desire to be included in the interdisciplinary process. Topics in art, according to the art teacher, could easily be correlated with topics in English, social studies, science, mathematics, and music.

Guide Questions

1. What subjects were included in the interdisciplinary process before the art teacher met with the principal?

2. What was the art teacher's perception of the planning process?

3. How did the principal help the art teacher see opportunities for being included in the process?

4. What should happen next?

In answering these questions, consider the perception of art, music, physical education, home economics, and technology education teachers toward the interdisciplinary team. One way of altering this perception is to identify ways to include all subjects in these interdisciplinary connections. Time for planning must be identified.

Case Study #7

During a parent conference, one teacher indicated an absence of the problems that other teachers were describing. As other teachers spoke about homework not being completed, quizzes not being made up, and book reports not being submitted, one teacher persistently said, "I do not have this problem in my classroom!" The impact of the statement was that the parent started to doubt the message of the team and/or to view the one teacher not describing these problems in a more favorable way.

Guide Questions

1. From this case study, what appears to be the major problem?

2. How will other teachers feel toward the teacher who indicated that there was no problem?

3. How will the parents feel about the teachers who see a problem as opposed to the one teacher who had no concerns?

4. How can such a problem be prevented?

5. In this specific case, what needs to happen next?

In answering these questions, consider the major underlying problem which may be a gap in communication between team members or the desire of one teacher to look good in the eyes of the parents. Some pre-planning should occur; and, if such a difference is identified, it needs to be resolved before the conference begins. Although a student may have various measures of success in various classrooms, a situation like the one described has the potential to create doubt in the minds of well-meaning, supportive parents.

Case Study #8

At a parent conference, one teacher dominates by providing extraneous details. Rather than helping the discussion move toward the identification of major problems, this teacher fixates on details related to that one classroom situation. As a result, the major purposes of the conference are not accomplished, and the parent questions the need for the conference. Additionally, the parent intensifies the blame on the teachers for the student's problems.

Guide Questions

1. Why did one teacher attempt to dominate the conference?

2. Why did that teacher avoid dealing with the problems of the student?

3. How should the other team members steer the conference to get it back on course?

4. At the next team meeting, what strategies might the other team members use to avoid a repetition of the problem?

In answering these questions, consider the needs of the teacher who attempted to dominate with extraneous details, other teachers on the team, and the parents. It is hoped that the team will be able to respond to the one teacher's problems before or after the parent conference. Because teaming is relatively new and parents may feel threatened, it is essential that the main purpose of the conference be accomplished.

Case Study #9

In a series of team planning meetings, the reading teacher visited the team to enlist the support of the teachers for the upcoming "Author's Day" program. Readiness for the visit of the author included reading some of the author's works aloud to students and planning for a series of assemblies for pupils to meet the author. As these planning sessions continued, it became apparent that some members of the team were not willing to take the time from their subject to read aloud to pupils and that other teachers were not willing to allow time for classes and individuals to attend assemblies and other special sessions with the author. Because of insight and experience, the reading teacher was able to help the team identify the real problem which was a lack of commitment to team activities. A series of discussions followed focusing on the role and function of the team.

Guide Questions

1. What were some of the clues that the reading teacher utilized in identifying the real problem?

2. What could have occurred if the real problem were not identified?

3. How can resource people (reading teacher, guidance counselor, administrators) help teams to identify real problems in a conflict situation?

4. What strategies might be used to help a team identify its commitment to team and school activities in addition to the time needed to teach the curriculum?

In answering these questions, consider the pressures on teachers to support various district, school, and team activities. Teachers naturally see themselves as the teacher of a subject area and are desirous for as much time as possible in that content area. The middle school concept asks teachers to be more than just a teacher of a subject area. A balance between team/school activities and completing the prescribed curriculum is desirable.

Case Study #10

In forming the agenda for a team meeting, one teacher asked for the opportunity to discuss a personal problem. As the discussion unfolded, the teacher expressed belief that the team process made her feel that she was under constant scrutiny by other members of the team. The teacher described feeling uncomfortable sharing ideas. This teacher never critiqued the ideas of other team members who had interpreted this as an indication of her not wishing to be challenged by others. When a team member asked a question about this issue, the teacher stormed out of the room in tears.

Guide Questions

1.   What prompted the teacher to place a personal problem on the agenda?

2.   What may have caused the teacher to feel uncomfortable?

3.   What responsibility or obligation do other team members have for the teacher expressing discomfort?

4.   Once the teacher left the meeting in tears, what should other team members do?

5.   How and when should the team resume discussion of this concern?

In answering these questions, consider the possibility that the problem has nothing to do with school. Also, consider the possibility that the person has no training in an interactive communication situation such as the team process. Part of the focus must be on the individual expressing these concerns, but a major portion of the focus has to be on establishing effective communication to accomplish team goals. In this situation, another team member may need to become the mentor or support the distressed teacher.

Case Study #11

Because of a resignation late in the summer, a new teacher was hired for a seventh grade English position on an interdisciplinary team. This teacher had graduated from college several years previously and did not feel fully prepared to function in a team setting. This teacher recognized how much needed to be learned and was given encouragement by every member of the team, the department head, and the reading teacher. As a result, the teacher became a contributing member of the interdisciplinary team and volunteered to attend several middle school conferences during the course of the school year in an effort to learn more about the middle school concept.

Guide Questions

1.   What responsibility does the interdisciplinary team have to help a first year teacher?

2.   To what extent is a mentoring system in operation?

3.   What staff development opportunities exist for non-tenured personnel?

In answering these questions, consider the fact that this was a success story. Without caring and nurturing teachers, the outcome could have been different. First year teachers have a lot to learn in terms of curriculum and the uniqueness of a given school. In some cases, they may not become contributing members of an interdisciplinary team. The difference lies in the quality and quantity of help provided by other staff members.

Case Study #12

Because of parallels in the schedule, two eighth grade teams have the identical schedule. Because of heterogeneous grouping, homogeneous grouping, a gifted and talented program, and integrating special education students into regular classes, there was considerable cross-team regrouping. Some teachers felt as though others had "preferred assignments." There was considerable competition, anger, and resentment.

Guide Questions

1. How are teams formed?

2. How are teacher assignments created?

3. To what extent is there an effort to have equity?

4. How can petty jealousies be resolved before they become more serious problems?

5. To what extent can the planning process be balanced to have team meetings, grade level meetings, and individual subject meetings?

In answering these questions, consider the balance in focusing on the needs of students as well as teachers. Teachers need help in accepting their assignments and working in a professional way to address student needs. Administrators must become involved when there are indications of interpersonal problems at the teachers' level.

Case Study #13

After returning from a bereavement leave, a teacher was unable to focus or concentrate on topics discussed at team meetings. The teacher was late for meetings and had numerous excuses for not fulfilling team responsibilities. Despite empathetic statements from various team members, the symptoms continued until such time that the teacher requested an extended medical leave.

Guide Questions

1. In what ways can out-of-school problems affect one's teaching performance?

2. In what ways can members of the teaching team be of assistance in a situation such as this?

3. What resources may a school or school district utilize to assist both the teacher and the teaching team?

In answering these questions, consider the extent to which out-of-school problems affect teaching. Teams are limited in the extent to which they can be of assistance. A referral for professional help may be necessary. The behaviors described or observed may be symptoms of a larger problem.

Case Study #14

The principal called a special meeting of an interdisciplinary team. At this meeting, the principal announced that several parents called the superintendent to report that confidential information about their children had reached the community. When questioned, several teachers candidly admitted telling friends about standardized test scores and IEP data. The group had a long discussion on the importance of being professional and maintaining confidentiality under any circumstance.

Guide Questions

1. Why would a teacher betray confidences?

2. What are the professional responsibilities of a teacher on a teaching team in terms of information learned at a team planning meeting?

3. What guidelines might a school district, school, or individual teaching team create on the subject of confidentiality?

In answering these questions, consider that betrayal of confidentiality is a symptom of a larger problem. Teachers must be professional; professionalism must include the team process as well as the routine classroom areas. Teachers lower the image of the school and school system when they act in unprofessional ways. All must work together to constantly upgrade the image of teachers, teaching, and all aspects of the middle school concept.

Case Study #15

As part of the master schedule, one special education teacher meets with a sixth grade interdisciplinary team twice per week. The teachers discuss handicapped students about to be placed in regular education classes. On a given day, the mathematics teacher began to complain vociferously, claiming that the class was entirely too large already and that the last two handicapped students placed in this section are now failing the course. Despite the efforts of the special education teacher to respond to the questions of the regular education teacher, the argument continued.

Guide Questions

1. What guidelines exist for integrating students with special needs into the regular program?

2. How can team planning periods be utilized as an opportunity for special education and regular education teachers to discuss mutual concerns?

3. In what ways can this integration process be evaluated?

4. How should this argument be resolved?

In answering these questions, consider the frustration of regular education teachers trying to meet the needs of handicapped students. Although class size is a factor, staff development is a greater issue. The master schedule can provide a definite time for all professionals concerned to focus on these problems. Guidelines for the least restrictive environment must be created, implemented, and ultimately evaluated.

SUMMARY

There will be conflicts among team members; these conflicts need to be resolved at the teachers' level in a highly professional, nurturing fashion. Fifteen case studies were provided in this chapter; teams should select several of these for further study as part of the team building process and/or staff development activities. Resolving conflict includes a focus on group dynamics, communications skills, respect, acceptance, professionalism, a belief in the team process, and time. Teams will need to and can grow in their capacity to resolve conflict.

12

Effective Leadership at the Team Level

Effective leadership is vital at the team level. Without direction, the team cannot achieve its full potential as an independent organism. This leadership must come from within the team. External sources such as the superintendent or building principal cannot provide the leadership needed for the day-to-day functioning of each team. A member of the team or all of the members of the team must accept responsibility for the team's success.

IMPORTANCE OF LEADERSHIP AT THE TEAM LEVEL

Every team is unique. No other team has the same teachers or same students. As a result, each team will have its own personality, strengths, and limitations. Each team must develop its own structure to accomplish its goals and purposes. As a result, every team should have a measure of local autonomy. Although there are regulations and guidelines for each school or department of instruction, teams are able to make many decisions within the framework or guidelines. Each team is responsible, in its own way, to respond to the needs of its students and deliver the prescribed program of studies.

Among the many local option functions for which the team normally has autonomy are: the initial grouping of students into teaching sections, regrouping pupils, correlating factual information in the various subjects, selecting particular skills for emphasis, creating a skills lab program, identifying topics for the home base program, scheduling parent conferences, and using modular scheduling techniques.

Leadership is needed at the team level to insure that such decisions are made properly and that the unique personality of the team emerges. Although these decisions should ultimately be reported to the building principal, they ought to be made by the individual team, not by the principal.

ROLE OF THE TEAM LEADER

A member of the team, usually designated as team leader, must be willing to accept responsibility for the following tasks:

Presiding over meetings. The team leader must chair the meeting and see that all agenda items are covered. Meetings must conclude on time so that teachers are able to continue with their other responsibilities.

Providing team building activities as needed. For the most part, team building activities are scheduled for the beginning of the school year or at a time of crisis for a team. The team leader may, however, decide to schedule certain team building activities periodically during the course of the year. Such an approach reinforces the developmental aspect of the team building process.

Involving all team members in discussions and meetings. Certain members of the team may be quiet or passive. Or, some members of the team may not sense the importance of the team process and choose not to actively participate in the discussions. At the other extreme, some team members may attempt to dominate discussions and/or manipulate the decision-making process. The team leader, therefore, must work to involve all members of the team equally. Open-ended questions can be used as a way of involving everyone.

Dealing with differences of opinion or divisiveness among team members when problems arise. It is only natural that there will be differences of opinion on certain topics. Team members should be encouraged to be honest in sharing their ideas. Good listeners listen carefully to the point of view of other team members to fully understand points of view and ultimately move toward consensus. The team leader must establish a spirit of acceptance so that people will resolve differences in identifying what is best for the students.

Accepting other group members. Acceptance is a key topic in the group process. Teachers may have preferences as to which members of the faculty they want to team with and which members of the faculty they would choose to exclude from their team. Obviously, it is not always possible to form all teams with all members who truly want to be with each other. It is necessary, therefore, to work at acceptance of other team members. The team leader is responsible for facilitating acceptance.

Developing an agenda for each meeting. The team leader is responsible for developing an agenda for each team meeting. The agenda must reflect the scope and sequence of the responsibilities of the team. A number of categories must be included on a regular, systematic basis.

Providing assistance for substitute teachers. There will be times when members of the teaching team are absent from school on a daily or long-term basis. It is imperative to involve substitute teachers in the team process as well as to utilize the strength of the team to help substitute teachers be successful. Especially in the case of long-term substitutes, the team must extend a welcome to these individuals, utilize their strengths wherever possible, and guarantee that the team process continues despite the absence of one of the members.

Facilitating the correlation of content as well as skills. From a cognitive point of view, a major responsibility of the team is to correlate content and skills on a regular basis. In many cases, this involves considerable discussion and consideration of what is best for the students in light of the time available to the team. The team leader must insure that the correlation of content and skills is a high priority item. Also, records should be kept of these decisions to minimize time needed for this process in subsequent years.

Handling the paperwork for the team or delegating that responsibility. Despite all efforts to the contrary, there will always be some paperwork related to the teaming process. The team planning log is a major report that teams are required to submit on a weekly basis. Other reports may be required as part of the accountability of time given to teachers for the planning process. In some cases, the team leader does all of the paperwork; in other cases, the team leader may delegate the responsibility.

Facilitating the evaluation of the team's functioning. In a later chapter, there is an extensive plan for evaluating the functioning of the team. The evaluation may be conducted at the end of each quarter or semester or on an as needed basis. The team leader has a major responsibility to see that the process occurs in an open and honest fashion. The major purpose of evaluation is to facilitate communication among team members.

Monitoring time limits during the team meeting. It is essential that time limits be adhered to for each item on the agenda. If parents are scheduled to meet with the team, these sessions should start and stop on time. Items scheduled for the latter part of the agenda are just as important as those items scheduled for the earlier part. The team leader should carefully monitor time limits to respect each item on that agenda.

Serving as the liaison between the administration and the team. The team leader has definite responsibilities to serve as the link between the administrators and members of the team. In these communications, it is important to represent the best interests of the entire team.

Meeting with the principal as requested or as needed. In addition to meeting with the principal along with other team leaders, time should be provided for the team leader to meet with the principal on a one-to-one basis. Again, the importance of the team in the total organization and culture of the school must be emphasized.

Monitoring the achievement of the team's goals. The team leader must periodically stop to evaluate the achievement of the team's goals. Unlike school, department, and personal teaching goals, the team's goals may be set and evaluated on a bi-weekly, monthly, or quarterly basis. Assessing current goals is an important prerequisite for establishing future goals.

Submitting reports and receiving communications for the team. The team leader must submit all reports for the team or delegate that responsibility. The team leader should also be the one to receive all communications from the administration, guidance department, and/or other resource personnel. Requests from parents to meet with the team may also be submitted to the team leader. This helps the team leader establish the agenda for team meetings.

Establishing consensus needed for decisions. A variety of techniques are needed to gain consensus once discussion has taken place. In some cases, the team leader will be able to gain consensus by simply reflecting upon the stated position of each team member on a particular issue. In other cases, the team leader may call for a vote to know precisely what each team member's feelings are.

Helping team members implement the middle school philosophy. There will be times when team members lose sight of the middle school philosophy as they pursue their own agenda items or become upset while discussing a particular agenda item. The team leader must help team members remember that the purposes of the team are to facilitate the instructional program and implement the philosophy and goals of the middle school program.

Informing special area teachers of team activities. As the interdisciplinary team plans various activities, it is important to keep special area teachers informed of these events. This builds morale within the school. As disciplinary and core/combination subject teams plan a variety of activities, they too should inform the interdisciplinary teams of these events.

Coordinating the involvement of resource personnel. In order to maximize time and human resources, the team leader must schedule various resource personnel who wish to attend team meetings. If the reading teacher would like to meet with the team, the reading teacher should contact the team leader. The team leader should extend invitations to various resource personnel. Teams must have their own identity and yet work effectively with all resource personnel; thus, coordination is mandatory.

Monitoring the effectiveness of decision-making processes within the team. Teams will utilize a variety of decision-making processes. In some cases, outspoken individuals will influence excessively the decision-making process. In other cases, the absence of thorough discussion will affect the decision-making process. The team leader must be very sensitive to decision-making processes and reflect this information to the total team. At times, it may be necessary to halt discussion of a certain topic to look at the decision-making process in effect. This is an important responsibility for the team leader.

Coordinating the planning for special events. As teams plan field trips, home base activities, and assemblies, the team leader must be sensitive to details. Even though another member of the team may be responsible for the event, the team leader must include this special event as an on-going agenda item.

Helping team members see opportunities for flexible scheduling and the need to regroup pupils. The techniques for flexible scheduling and regrouping students for various instructional purposes must be implemented by each team on an individual basis. As needed, the team leader must help other team members recognize the potential of these strategies. In many ways, the team leader becomes a teacher who is introducing a new skill.

Being certain that all team members see the relationship between planning periods and the instructional program. As needed, the team leader must be certain that team members see the relationship between team planning periods and the instructional program.

Utilizing sub-groupings of the team when appropriate. There will be times when the team leader or one member of the team suggests that it is not necessary for all team members to be involved in a certain discussion or task. The team leader should then recognize the opportunity to utilize a subgrouping, designate the members of the subgroup, state the task of the subgroup, and schedule a specific time for the subgroup to provide a report for the total team.

Obviously, the team leader has a very important responsibility. The team leader must insure that the team functions to the best of its potential by involving all team members in the process and providing students with the best possible instructional program.

SHARING THE LEADERSHIP RESPONSIBILITY

It is not essential that the team leader serve for the entire school year or that one person be expected to be responsible for all of the leadership responsibilities. In some middle schools, the team leader is awarded a salary supplement and serves the entire year. In other situations, the team leader is appointed by the principal and receives no additional remuneration. It is not necessary for the team leader to be a quasi-administrator or quasi-instructional supervisor. The team leader should be a peer or equal of the other team members. Since a large middle school may have 10-20 different teams in operation, it would not be feasible to have that many people with administrative/supervisory responsibility factors, paid or unpaid.

The team leader can be chosen by the members of each teaching team or the position can be rotated. A four member interdisciplinary team can, for example, decide to rotate the position of team leader every nine weeks among all four members. When this happens, every team member has a greater respect for the leadership responsibility.

Some teams have asked certain members to specialize in various facets of the team process. For instance, one member may coordinate the skills program, a second person may handle the preparation of materials for the home base program, a third team member may handle scheduling and regrouping responsibilities, and the fourth person may publish the bi-weekly team newsletter. Remaining leadership tasks may rotate among the members. The result is an acceptance of the leadership function by all team members. It is not always necessary or wise to "burden" one team member with all aspects of team leadership.

SUMMARY

There must be effective leadership at the team level for the team to function to the best of its potential. Many specific functions are assigned to the team leader whether appointed by the principal or selected by peers. It is also possible for all team members to serve as team leader for a portion of the school year. When all team members share the experience of being team leader, they have a greater appreciation of the leadership function in the team process.

Activity:

1. How will team leaders be chosen in our school?

2. What is the role of the team leader?

3. To what extent can the role of team leader be shared?

4. How will team leadership be evaluated in our school?

13

Evaluating the Effectiveness of the Team

Teaching teams utilize the combined skills, talents, interests, and training of teachers from one or more disciplines. In order for teams to function effectively, these components must mesh smoothly. As a result, there is the need for some instrument to help team members assess the effectiveness of the team process.

WHO SHOULD EVALUATE?

The issue of who should conduct the evaluation is a very important one. Within the educational arena, a number of agencies and/or persons are typically involved in evaluating teachers, teaching, and the curriculum -- regional accrediting consortia or agencies, state accrediting groups, teams from individual school districts, principals, and/or peers from the school or school district. The responsibility for evaluating the effectiveness of individual teaching teams could be added to such groups' concerns.

Each of these groups could approach the assessment process with a list of goals, objectives, and guidelines. Since these might or might not reflect the priorities, experiences, strengths, or limitations of a specific teaching team, each teaching team could conduct a self-evaluation. Outsiders might not be sufficiently familiar with the team process or the specific situation to evaluate effectively.

Thus, self-evaluation may be the most appropriate form of evaluation because it involves close introspection by the members of the team using a form that parallels the philosophy, practices, and uniqueness of that particular team. A self-evaluation involves an open sharing of feelings about the activities of a team and facilitates channeling this discussion into constructive goal-setting activities.

DEVELOPING AN INSTRUMENT

Although a sample is included, the structure of an instrument could be determined by the State Department of Education, local school district, individual middle level school, or individual teaching team. The instrument should be used regularly, systematically, and in a positive fashion. Most importantly, the instrument should facilitate communication between team members.

All of the questions in the example below do not need to be included. From this rather lengthy list, items could be selected that are most meaningful to the individual team. Other questions that reflect the priorities, goals, or experiences of team members could be added.

Evaluating the Effectiveness of the Team

	Consis-tently	Fre-quently	Occa-sionally	Comment
1. Does the team respond to needs of students?				
2. Does the team enhance the self-concept of students?				
3. Do members of the team discuss their commitment to the middle school concept?				
4. Do members of the team explore their role and function as a team?				
5. Do members of the team make an effort to know each other?				
6. Do members of the team discuss their expectations of each other?				
7. Does the team work effectively with resource personnel?				

	Consis-tently	Fre-quently	Occa-sionally	Comment
8. Do members of the team support the efforts of the team leader				
9. Are efforts made to resolve conflicts among team members?				
10. Are leadership res-ponsibilities shared?				
11. Does everyone participate equally in making decisions?				
12. Are guidelines for gaining consensus for decision-making followed?				
13. Have team decisions been implemented?				
14. Are records kept of team decisions?				
15. Are there specific goals and objectives for the year?				
16. Does the team evaluate goals and objectives periodically?				
17. Do team members correlate content between subjects included on the team?				
18. Do team members correlate the teaching of skills?				
19. Are skills taught in context?				
20. Does the team provide a home base program for students?				
21. Do team members recognize relation-ship of planning periods to instruc-tional program?				
22. Do team members use varied techniques in communicating with parents?				
23. Are parent con-ferences successful?				

	Consistently	Frequently	Occasionally	Comment
24. Does the team strive to include special education students within the team process?				
25. Do team members utilize opportunities for modular/flexible scheduling?				
26. Do team members develop and utilize rotating schedules?				
27. Do team members identify local options available to the team?				
28. Do team members develop plans to use local options?				
29. Do team members utilize opportunities to group and regroup pupils for various instructional purposes?				
30. Do team members use available data about pupils in developing overall instructional program?				
31. Are individual team members sensitive to group dynamics at team meetings?				
32. Does the team have an agenda for all meetings?				
33. Is agenda followed?				
34. Is team planning time kept strictly for team business?				
35. Does the team utilize sub-groupings of the team when appropriate?				
36. Do team members offer suggestions for the design of the master schedule?				
37. Do team members participate in staff development activities?				

	Consistently	Frequently	Occasionally	Comment
38. Do students benefit from the team's efforts?				
39. Do team members discuss appropriate teaching strategies?				
40. Do team members assess team planning logs on regular basis?				
41. Are opportunities for alternate day rotations utilized?				
42. Is paper work completed in a timely fashion?				

USE OF THE INSTRUMENT

Members of the team should look at the questions objectively, and each member should record the answer to each of the questions. This could be done during a team meeting or as "homework." The team leader or an impartial outsider (guidance counselor, principal, assistant principal, department head) could help the team arrive at consensus.

It is important to identify areas of agreement as well as areas of disagreement. It is important to know, for example, that all five members of the team felt that the team responds to the needs of students consistently. Beyond agreeing on the response, team members should tell why they responded as they did. This discussion might reveal several factors more important to the team than knowing all checked the column "consistently."

On the other hand, a diversity of responses is healthy. In answering the question, "Does the team work effectively with resource personnel?," two members may say *frequently* while two members indicate *occasionally*. Rather than trying to get one team member to change the response to reach a majority, it is more important to find out why members responded the way they did.

In the discussion, factors may emerge that are important in gaining insight into the situation. For example, team members may feel that they work well with the reading teacher but not with the guidance counselor. The issue could be the expectations that team members have of resource personnel. The reading teacher may be willing to create lesson plans or mini-units for the teachers of the team while the guidance counselor feels that all should work together in helping a student having some difficulty.

Assessment should enhance communication. Self-evaluation is a means of getting team members together to examine what they are doing, how they could improve, and how some priorities for improvement would be established. The most important outcome is communication. Team members should work together to plan for improvement. Team goals can emerge naturally from the assessment process.

SUMMARY

Teaching teams should evaluate their efforts as a team. A process was suggested in this chapter that will help to gauge the skills necessary for a team to operate successfully. The assessment process is a means to the end of effective communication among team members about the team, its role, and its function.

Activity:

1. Who will evaluate the effectiveness of our team?

2. Will we have the opportunity to participate in a self-evaluation as part of the overall plan for evaluation? If so, how?

3. What instrument will we use to evaluate the effectiveness of our team? How will the instrument be used?

4. Can we use some or all of the items included in "Evaluating the Effectiveness of the Team?" Which are more relevant for us? Which are less relevant?

14

Appropriate Teaching Strategies

A discussion of how early adolescent students learn would be incomplete without a section focusing on appropriate teaching strategies. The strategies suggested in this chapter are appropriate for all teachers of all subjects. These constructs are not a function of the team approach to instruction; they are a response to the unique learning needs of early adolescent students. In schools where teachers are involved in team planning but not team teaching, these techniques should be discussed or explored as a part of the planning process. These approaches should be used on a daily basis in every classroom in every middle level school. Time should be included in team planning periods to discuss appropriate teaching strategies. Thus, team meetings can focus on methodology in addition to the teaming process and the teaching of specific content areas.

A RESPONSE TO LEARNING NEEDS

Current research on early adolescent development is the basis of these teaching postulates. Early adolescence is a period of great physical growth with pupils at various stages of development. Middle level educators must recognize individual differences. Early adolescents not only have a short attention span but also a low tolerance for fatigue.

Students in grades 6, 7, and 8 are also at various stages of intellectual and moral development. Some will leave middle school without ever moving past Piaget's concrete stage. Other students will begin to approach Piaget's formal thinking stage during grades 7 and 8. Teachers must be constantly aware of their responsibilities for teaching skills and processes in addition to the content. Teachers should always start lessons with concrete examples and move from the concrete to the abstract.

In addition to understanding and responding to extensive physical and intellectual maturation, teachers must be aware of the implications of social-emotional growth patterns. Students need to understand the changes taking place in their bodies and minds. Adults must be careful not to reinforce feelings of inadequacy. Hands-on activities will provide a better basis for the retention of knowledge. As teachers plan for instruction, they must always keep in the forefront of their thinking the importance of group membership, self-concept, peer approval, and independence from adults. Lessons that reinforce these ideas are in fact responding to the learning needs of the students.

Alexander's curriculum model is also a basis for many of these teaching strategies. Teachers working in teams should correlate content so pupils can see the wholeness of learning. Via association, pupils can link one idea to another and thus be better able to retain those ideas for longer periods of time. Skill development is important in each content area as well as a function of the interdisciplinary team. Skill development is reinforced when all teachers work in unison. Finally, the home base or teacher advisory program should be reinforced in the context of the entire instructional process.

Learning must be viewed as an active process, not a passive one. Students will remember what they did. Further, appropriate learning strategies for the early adolescent must be geared to the individuality of the student and the unique learning style of that individual. Curriculum guides must offer suggestions to teachers as to how to best teach the material to students in a given grade. Learning must be viewed as an active process in mathematics and English classes as well as in technology education, art, or physical education.

The remainder of this chapter will be divided into three parts. The first segment will present strategies that should be utilized by every teacher in every subject. The second segment will offer techniques that may be utilized under certain conditions in every content area. Finally, there will be some suggestions for improving the nature of the learning environment for the early adolescent. The strategy list is not meant to be inclusive. A continuing goal of every professional should be to enlarge the repertoire of strategies used on a regular basis.

AN APPROACH TO DAILY LESSON PLANNING

As teachers plan for instruction for every lesson for every day, the following teaching strategies are suggested to best meet the learning needs of early adolescent students.

1. **Plan lessons that divide the entire period (40 to 50 minutes) into four or five modules or segments of 10 to 15 minutes each.**

In preparing for instruction, a physical education teacher might subdivide a class period into a number of smaller units of time. In the first eight to ten minutes of the period, students change from their regular school clothing to physical education attire. Pupils, for the next five minutes, assemble in the gymnasium and participate in appropriate warm-up exercises.

After re-assembling in instructional groups, the teacher might demonstrate a new skill in the basketball unit. Following this demonstration, pupils would spend ten minutes practicing the new skill in small groups. For the next thirteen minutes, pupils would follow a round-robin format to integrate a number of skills in the basketball unit. For the next four minutes, the teacher would re-assemble the instructional group for a summary and assessment of the skill development process. The final eight minutes would be devoted to showering and dressing in regular school clothes for the remainder of the school day.

In mathematics, the class period might be divided as follows:

8:40-8:50   Pupils arrive and work on a drill on multiplication of decimals

8:50-8:55   Teacher checks the drill; pupils assess their performance

8:55-9:02   Homework is checked; pupils assess their performance on this activity

9:02-9:15   Teacher introduces new work on the multiplication of decimals; pupils participate in an inductive process and help to write the rule for multiplying decimals

9:15-9:25   Students complete classwork activity based on new skill presented; work is checked

9:25-9:28   Students participate in a summary of the lesson; students answer teacher's questions related to the skill, concept, and application

9:28-9:30   Teacher assigns homework and dismisses class

In these two examples, teachers subdivided the time available into a number of modules. The modules were of varying length and clearly depended upon the specific activities to be completed. The same general approach can and should be utilized in all subject areas.

2. Provide clear, concise structure for all activities.

In all subject areas, pupils must know exactly what to do for each specific activity. A foreign language teacher planning a vocabulary activity must review directions orally and also write them on the chalkboard so that students may refer to these directions while completing the activity in the event a question arises.

As teachers plan lessons, they must anticipate the kinds of questions students will ask as they complete the activity. Instructions should be given on a step-by-step basis. Teachers should not assume that all students can see the interrelationships between these steps.

Flow charts are helpful when teachers present a series of tasks to students. Early adolescent students can perform a variety of assignments when teachers give clear, concise, specific directions to students and when the number of items is not excessive.

3. Provide variety within the period.

As teachers organize instruction for 40 or 50 minutes of the lesson, they must provide variety so that students are not performing one continuous learning task. In foreign language, for instance, the lesson can include a vocabulary activity, an oral grammar activity, a written grammar activity, and a culture activity. Variety is achieved when various phases of the foreign language program are accomplished within the given period and there is a balance of oral and written activities.

A teacher of English can also provide for variety by planning four segments that could include a written grammar drill, a listening activity related to the grammar program, a writing activity related to the literature program, and an opportunity for sustained silent reading. Again, variety is achieved by subdividing time, by alternating activities between written and oral, by addressing all phases of the English curriculum, and correlating the various elements of that curriculum into a meaningful whole.

Teachers of all subject areas must recognize the importance of providing variety to sustain interest and enthusiasm of students. The need for variety is closely related to attention span limitations of students. This is important in terms of time, types of activities, and the interrelationship of elements of the curriculum. By recognizing the importance of variety, middle school teachers are responding to a major learning need of the early adolescent.

4. Clarify purposes for each activity.

Pupils must know exactly why they are asked to complete a certain activity. The social studies teacher must tell the students why they are completing a map to show the route of the Lewis and Clark Expedition. The science teacher, in preparing students to do a lab experiment, must review the importance of safety so students can practice safety habits as they work with the Bunsen burner. In mathematics, pupils must know the importance of studying percent.

Once students know these purposes, they are more willing to participate in activities. More importantly, they are able to assess their performance in relationship to these purposes. Without a stated purpose, students are not aware of the importance of a given activity and may not show the necessary enthusiasm for completing that activity.

5. Provide adequate motivation, readiness, and goal-setting.

Once purposes are established, teachers must make an overt effort to enhance motivation and readiness to ensure that students have the necessary prerequisites for learning. A specific effort to get the interest of pupils in the lesson topic is often needed. For example, a lesson in social studies could start with a picture as the motivational activity; the technology education teacher could show pupils an example of the finished product as a motivating device. Realia, pictures, maps, and items from the daily newspaper frequently serve as motivational devices.

It is important for teachers to monitor students' responses to the motivational activity. In developing the lesson, teachers must make an effort to relate the motivational activity to purposes of the lesson. This is most frequently accomplished by pre-planning several key questions to establish this relationship.

Readiness is similar to motivation and yet in some ways is different. Generally, the teacher is working to prepare the student to learn new material. Effective readiness in the middle grades includes preparation for both content and skill. A social studies teacher who is providing motivation and readiness for a reading selection on the causes of the Civil War would prepare students for the content material in the textbook and would also prepare youngsters for a skill such as reading for main ideas or cause and effect relationships. Readiness for content and skill could be accomplished concurrently.

Both motivation and readiness are part of a larger concept entitled goal-setting. Instruction for middle level students must be goal-oriented; both long and short range goals are essential. Teachers, as they organize a unit of study, must list both long and short range goals and, more importantly, plan lessons to include short range goals that help to achieve long range goals.

6. Utilize recall strategies.

Middle level teachers must make a special effort to utilize recall strategies. Recall strategies help the student to connect material to be learned with material already learned. For example, the current lesson should begin with several questions that summarize or review the lesson of the previous day. Teachers must remember that 24 hours or more have passed since the student was last in that classroom. The student attended six other classes since yesterday's lesson. Students also participated in many events outside of school. Recall, therefore, is essential.

Recall is effectively accomplished via a series of open-ended questions that help the student see connections between prior learning and goals of the current lesson. Drill questions and checking homework are other strategies to accomplish recall. An effort also must be made to help students who were absent for the previous lesson to quickly receive a synopsis of that lesson.

7. Provide transitions to connect various activities within the lesson.

An effective lesson for middle school students consists of several activities designed to accomplish a specific goal or goals. Although the teacher may easily see the relationship between these activities, it is essential that students recognize relationships. Thus, transitions should be used to make connections evident to students.

A transition consists of a summary statement of the previous activity, a preview of the next activity, and a statement of the relationship between the two parts. The approach should be inductive whenever possible. An English teacher might complete a discussion of the character study and then make a transition to a written activity related to a major literary theme. Via questions, students will be able to participate in the summary of the character studied, gain a preview of the literary theme, and be able to describe that relationship. There must be a transition between every activity in every lesson so that pupils are always aware of the relationship between the parts.

8. Be flexible within the structure.

Middle school teachers need to be structured. Effective middle school teachers spend a considerable amount of time planning lessons that properly challenge middle grades students.

Yet, within this structure, teachers need to be flexible. Questions may arise, and it will become apparent that some deviation from this plan or structured approach is vital. A student may ask a question that must be answered. A group of students may not fully comprehend a concept, and thus it is necessary to reteach that concept. It is also possible that students' frustration level is so great that the teacher needs to inject some humor in the lesson or perhaps delay an activity until a more appropriate time.

Another example of the need to be flexible is when a conflict arises in the cafeteria or corridors, and class time needs to be devoted to resolving that conflict so that students can continue with the primary task of learning. Effective middle school teachers must be flexible within a structured approach to teaching.

9. Know the cognitive level of students.

Just as teachers are aware of the reading and IQ levels of students whom they teach, effective middle school teachers should also be aware of cognitive levels or brain growth stages of each student.

Students in grades 6, 7, and 8 may be at one of the following stages of cognitive development: pre-operational, concrete onset, concrete mature, formal onset, or formal mature. Obviously some testing or screening using materials such as those developed by Michael Shayer, Patricia Arlin or others will be necessary to help teachers identify these levels. This information should not, however, be used as part of an effort to group students homogeneously for instruction.

Teachers should, on the other hand, call upon students at appropriate times in light of cognitive levels. It is helpful to direct the more concrete questions to students who may be at pre-operational or concrete onset. Questions that involve more abstract thinking should be asked of those who are at concrete mature, formal onset, or formal mature stages.

Teachers also have a responsibility to help expand cognitive levels of students. Answering higher order questions will help students to expand their thinking. The maturation process is long and arduous; some students may never reach formal mature. Nevertheless, effective middle school teachers should recognize cognitive levels of individual students, ask questions that are appropriate to that level of development, and generally be committed to helping students expand as possible.

10. **Move from concrete to abstract in the concept development process.**

As teachers begin lessons or, more specifically, as teachers start activities within lessons, concrete examples should be offered. Lessons should move from the concrete or specific to the abstract or more general and theoretical.

Concrete examples are specific and exact. A picture, model, advertisement, or slide can be used to begin the thought process. Teachers should enable students to see, feel, or touch these concrete examples. Teachers should also ask knowledge and comprehension questions to assess students' understanding of concrete examples.

As the lesson or activity continues, students should move toward the abstract. Examples of abstract ideas include democracy, communism, photosynthesis, associative law, irony, and nuclear energy. In guiding student comprehension and learning, teachers must move slowly and assess student comprehension at regular intervals. Students need help in applying ideas in new but similar situations. Ehrenberg point out that, "One who has conceptualized...is able to consistently identify new examples, create new examples, distinguish examples from non-examples, change non-examples into examples, and in every case, is able to explain what he/she has done by citing the presence or absence of the concept characteristics."

The Cognitive Level Matching project (CLM) in the Shoreham-Wading River School District was designed to teach teachers about child development theory and help teachers design teaching strategies for integrating these principles into their teaching. Teachers are taught to assess cognitive levels of students, cognitive demands of curriculum and, where discrepancies exist, create a better, more appropriate match. The program is based on the premise that students do not achieve because of frustrations that develop as a result of being subjected to curriculum that is inappropriately matched to their cognitive ability. Teachers who are aware of cognitive levels of students and who plan lessons that move from the concrete to the abstract are, in effect, working toward the same aims as the CLM program.

11. Construct effective questions to accomplish objectives of the lesson.

In preparation for instruction, teachers should plan certain key questions and list them in the formal lesson plan. The questions should be open-ended and designed to increase students' critical and creative thinking abilities. As teachers reflect upon their questioning techniques, they should answer the following questions on a self-assessment basis.

Are my questions clear and concise?

Do they help to achieve the objectives of the lesson?

Do I ask one question at a time?

Do I ask each question only once?

Do my questions elicit concepts as well as facts?

Do I call upon a student after the question has been asked?

As teachers analytically answer these questions, they will be working toward the improvement of questioning techniques.

Teachers should also recognize that there are levels of questions and that these levels reflect Bloom's Taxonomy. Questions can be considered on six levels as exemplified on this checklist developed by the M.O.S.T. (Mobile On Site Training) Unit in Baltimore County, Maryland (1983).

QUESTIONS CHECKLIST

I will ask questions in my lesson today that require my students to utilize various levels of thinking in answering the questions. The students will be able to demonstrate:

Knowledge Level
_____ know common terms
_____ know specific facts
_____ know methods and procedures
_____ know basic concepts
_____ know principles

Comprehension Level

_____ understand facts and principles
_____ draw conclusions
_____ interpret material
_____ translate verbal material to mathematical formulas
_____ estimate consequences implied in data
_____ justify methods and procedures

Application Level

_____ apply principles to new situations
_____ solve mathematical problems
_____ demonstrate correct usage of a procedure

Analysis Level

_____ analyze the organizational structure of a work
_____ recognize unstated assumptions
_____ recognize logical fallacies in reasoning
_____ distinguish between facts and inferences
_____ evaluate relevancy of data

Synthesis Level

_____ write a well organized theme, speech, and/or story
_____ propose a plan for an experiment
_____ integrate learning from several different areas into a plan for solving a problem
_____ formulate a new scheme for classifying objects

Evaluate Level

_____ judge the value of work by internal and/or external criteria
_____ judge the consistency of written material
_____ judge the adequacy with which conclusions are supported by data

Questions are often the key to the success of a lesson. Teachers must critically evaluate their skills in asking questions according to the specific objectives of a lesson or activity. Questions play a major factor in moving from the concrete to the abstract and facilitating learning.

12. Use wait-time effectively.

Wait-time is defined as the length of the silent period following the asking of a question and prior to the initial student response to that question. Wait-time also includes the time between a student response and the next response. The average teacher waits for an answer for only one second. A longer wait-time has been found to have a positive effect on the quality of teacher-pupil interaction and achievement in science lessons. Teachers should extend pauses before beginning explanations, giving directions, asking questions, or reacting to pupil talk. These pauses give students additional time to formulate an answer, and thus there is a greater chance for students to participate in the ensuing discussion. By increasing wait-time to five seconds, teachers may anticipate the following results: (1) student responses lengthen, (2) whole sentence replies are given, (3) student questions increase, (4) teacher expectations of students are revised, and (5) teacher questions show more variability.

13. **Teach reading skills as part of an organized, systematic process.**

All middle school teachers are or should be teachers of reading. Throughout the school year, every teacher should make an effort to teach the following reading skills in the context of that subject.

READING SKILLS - MIDDLE SCHOOL

A. Vocabulary
 1. Shows knowledge of basic sight vocabulary
 2. Uses context as a clue to word meaning
 3. Uses phonics skills as an aid to pronunciation and word meaning
 4. Breaks down words into syllables as an aid to pronunciation and word meaning
 5. Uses prefixes, suffixes, and roots as an aid to word meaning
 6. Understands multiple meanings
 7. Understands figurative expressions (e.g., idioms, similes, and metaphors)
 8. Understands pronoun references
 9. Understands word relationships (e.g., antonyms, synonyms, and homonyms)
 10. Understands use of the dictionary to obtain word meanings and pronunciations
 11. Distinguishes between concrete and abstract terms
 12. Classifies items and terms

B. Comprehension
 1. Recalls details for various purposes
 2. Determines sequential order
 3. Finds the main idea of a passage
 4. Identifies ideas implied but not directly stated
 5. Understands relationships (e.g., time, place, cause and effect, and analogies)
 6. Interprets mood of a situation, story, or poem
 7. Draws conclusions and predicts outcomes
 8. Distinguishes between fact and opinion
 9. Recognizes mass persuasion techniques
 10. Generalizes comparisons and contrasts

C. Study Skills
 1. Uses parts of a book
 2. Uses reference books and periodicals
 3. Uses library resources to obtain information
 4. Takes notes about a topic

5. Makes an outline to summarize information
6. Identifies author's attitude and purpose
7. Evaluates information for validity
8. Adjusts rate of reading according to type of material and purpose

D . Functional Reading
1. Follows directions
2. Locates information
3. Gains information using main ideas
4. Gains information using details
5. Understands forms
6. Selects reading as a personal activity

E . Oral Reading
1. Uses oral intonation patterns
2. Uses punctuation as a clue to the proper reading of a sentence
3. Uses voice to interpret feelings and moods of characters
4. Uses correct phrasing

Adapted from: *Planning for Reading Instruction K-6*
Baltimore County Public Schools (1979)

In addition to developing a comprehensive perspective of the reading skills to be taught in grades 6, 7, and 8, middle school faculties should develop a consistent approach for teaching directed reading lessons. This format should be utilized in all subject areas and include the following elements: (1) motivation/readiness for the content as well as the skill, (2) vocabulary development, (3) setting of specific purpose(s) for silent reading, (4) silent reading, (5) discussion of purpose questions, and (6) follow-up activities.

14. Provide opportunities for guided practice sessions.

As students master content in a variety of settings, teachers must provide opportunities for guided practice, including modeling and structured feedback by the teacher. Students must be held accountable for information and skills learned. Additionally, students must be able to apply this learning in a variety of contexts. Guided practice is essential in this mastery process.

15. Incorporate activities which develop students' critical thinking skills.

As individuals and members of teaching teams, teachers must identify ways to incorporate activities in the daily curriculum which develop students' critical and creative thinking, decision-making, and problem solving abilities. This topic must be viewed as a critical need of the early adolescent learner as well as an aspect of mastering content.

16. **Use teaching strategies which are appropriate to the diverse learning styles of students.**

All students do not learn in the same way. Teachers can no longer rationalize a student's poor performance; they must be held accountable for knowing the unique learning styles of each student and providing a variety of approaches to ensure that every student has equal access to a successful learning experience.

17. **Provide a summary or assessment.**

There should be a summary and/or assessment at the end of each activity as well as at the end of a lesson. Assessment can be achieved via a specified activity or a series of directed questions. The assessment or summary should help pupils recognize what they learned during that lesson as well as what will happen next in the learning process. Assessment can be on a group as well as an individual basis. Pupils should anticipate what will happen next in the learning process. All student questions and concerns should be addressed prior to dismissing a class.

UNIQUE STRATEGIES FOR CERTAIN CONDITIONS

In the previous section, a number of strategies were suggested that can be utilized by every teacher in every subject area. In the next segment, additional strategies designed to meet unique needs of early adolescent students will be presented. In contrast with earlier suggestions, these may only be applicable for certain subjects or in certain situations.

1. **Facilitate student-to-student interaction.**

Traditional secondary teaching has been characterized by a pattern of teacher statement followed by student statement. Teachers ask a question, students answer a question, and then teachers ask the next question.

Lomax and Cooley (1981) found that there were interesting differences in achievement outcomes when students spend a great deal of time discussing, answering questions, listening, and engaging in other types of classroom interactive activities. The middle school classroom should feature many opportunities for student-to-student interaction through cooperative learning strategies as a response to the learning needs of the early adolescent. Students should interact with one another on mathematics problems, science laboratory experiments, building charts and graphs in social studies, and discussing the plot of a novel in English. Whenever possible, the classroom activity should permit physical movement to reduce the restlessness that characterizes this age group.

2. Assign team tasks.

Team or small group tasks are an extension of student-to-student interaction and usually involve groups of students working on specific academic tasks. This approach is a response to the social-emotional development of the early adolescent and must be carefully supervised by the teacher to keep the competitive aspect in control. This can be highly motivational for the student who needs peer pressure to perform. The focus should clearly be on the group rather than on the individual. Teachers of all subject areas are encouraged to find opportunities for small group tasks.

3. Utilize a team approach to skill development.

When teachers are working on interdisciplinary teams, they should work together in a skill-of-the-week program. In addition to teaching skills in each subject area, students benefit from the motivation and reinforcement of a unified approach. While it is more difficult to correlate content on a regular basis, students clearly see the benefits of this approach to skill development.

4. Create simulation and game techniques.

Early adolescent students thoroughly enjoy opportunities for simulations and games within the structure of the classroom. Social studies teachers have numerous opportunities to create simulations to teach topics in history, economics, or sociology. Technology education teachers utilize the assembly line process as an excellent simulation. Home economics teachers use numerous simulation approaches for teaching family life topics as well as decision-making.

These simulations and games give students a chance to experience the topic being discussed. After the simulation or game experience has been completed, the teacher should ask numerous questions to help students comprehend and analyze that which occurred. Real learning takes place in the post-simulation discussion. A number of educational games are available commercially and are applicable to the middle grades curriculum.

5. Use the inductive method.

Much teaching at the secondary level is of a deductive nature and involves the teacher explaining to students the rule or principle in effect. On the other hand, inductive teaching allows students to discover the rule by examining data or examples and answering a number of key questions presented by the teacher. For example, an English teacher may present a grammar rule on punctuating items in a series by having a number of sentences on the chalkboard or overhead projector that need to be punctuated. Via a careful questioning approach by the teacher, pupils will discover where to place the commas and why the commas were or were not in certain places. This process culminates with the writing of a rule which is really a summary of the learning experience provided. Topics in mathematics, science, foreign language, and other subject areas can be presented inductively. Information learned inductively is retained longer than materials presented deductively.

6. Allow independent study.

As a supplement to traditional classroom instruction, middle school students benefit from opportunities for independent study. Independent study allows students to move at their own pace, explore areas of interest, or work with a group of peers on a project of mutual interest. Independent study is intended to supplement traditional instruction, not replace it.

7. Include peer teaching/peer counseling.

Middle school students can be used as peer teachers and peer counselors. Students can conduct certain parts of the lesson such as checking the drill or homework as well as preparing materials and/or a mini-lecture for their peers on a given topic. Students can also play a major role in group counseling activities by serving as the group leader. Teachers and guidance counselors ought to find additional ways for peer teaching and peer counseling as a constructive response to the social-emotional development of early adolescents.

8. Provide enrichment for formal thinkers.

Students who are capable of handling higher levels of abstraction should receive the necessary challenges. Since most students require more concrete approaches, instruction must be aimed at the majority. Every teacher, therefore, has responsibility to find appropriate ways of challenging formal thinkers. This can be accomplished by reserving certain questions for these students, letting them do independent study, and assigning supplementary work.

NATURE OF THE LEARNING ENVIRONMENT

The final section on appropriate teaching strategies will include suggestions for improving the nature of the learning environment for the early adolescent.

1. Decorate classrooms appropriate to subject(s) being taught and age(s) of student(s).

The environment of the middle school classroom should be an extension of the elementary classroom. Bulletin boards should reflect topics of study as well as other items of importance to students of that age group. Mobiles and plants add to the environment of the classroom and team area. The goal is to establish an inviting environment for learning.

2.   Utilize flexible scheduling techniques.

Pupils benefit when flexible scheduling is used. Members of the interdisciplinary team should identify opportunities for flexible scheduling and utilize those whenever possible. All lessons do not have to be for fifty minutes; special activities can be scheduled to supplement traditional curriculum.

3.   Anticipate and prevent problems.

In planning a lesson, field trip, or special activity for the team, teachers should anticipate potential problems and then work to prevent them. Anticipation of problems is a fundamental part of the planning process.

4.   Encourage risk-taking.

Middle school students grow when they have the opportunity to take risks in a secure, protected environment. Risk-taking can occur in a reading class, physical education class, or science lab. Students, although initially leery of taking a risk, will take that chance when the student-teacher rapport is positive. A caring teacher encourages students to take risks. Students learn when they take risks in a positive fashion.

5.   Focus on affective issues.

In addition to presenting content material to students, middle school teachers should also address affective or emotional topics that arise in the course of the learning process. The science teacher may need to take a few minutes from the explanation of a scientific principle to resolve an altercation between two students in that classroom. A student who may have experienced some abuse at home may feel comfortable sharing that with a teacher. A discussion of a novel in English may prompt a student to share some personal experience with either the class as a whole, a small group of students within that classroom, or with that teacher on a one-to-one basis. Teachers should be concerned with affective issues, not just their subject matter.

6.   Inject humor whenever possible.

Teachers need to find opportunities to inject humor into the lesson. Even "silly jokes" are appreciated by students and help students to remember the content material. Humor should always be in good taste and never at the expense of a student or another faculty member.

7.   Praise, don't criticize.

Like adults, middle school students respond best to praise. Teachers must take the time to find ways to praise students in a manner that is accepted and respected by the student receiving praise as well as others in the classroom. Teachers must use a variety of terms in dispensing this praise so as not to make the words seem too mechanical. Teachers are quick to point out shortcomings of their students; on the other hand, teachers and teams should find ways to inform parents of students' positive accomplishments. The appropriate use of praise reinforces and facilitates learning.

SUMMARY

Current research on the development of the early adolescent student suggests a number of appropriate teaching strategies. This chapter presented suggestions that can be utilized in daily lesson plans, under certain conditions, and can enhance both the physical and emotional aspects of the learning environment. Middle level teachers must assess themselves to identify which strategies they are already using and which can be added to their repertoire.

Activity:

1. As an individual, which of these strategies am I already using?

2. As an individual, which of these strategies would I like to add to my repertoire?

3. As a team, which of these strategies are we using sufficiently?

4. Which additional strategies would enhance our effectiveness as a team?

5. What staff development activities would help our team and faculty grow professionally?

15

Staff Development

Staff development is an essential element in the successful implementation of the team process. Prior to embarking on this broad topic, there must be a focus on the change process itself. Educational leaders must be fully aware of dynamics involved in creating change. Beyond writing goals and objectives, there must be a clear focus on how people involved will be affected, respond to changes, and ultimately facilitate the change process.

FULLAN'S MODEL FOR THE CHANGE PROCESS

In a review of the effective schools research, Michael Fullan (1985) focuses on the implications of these data in terms of change strategy. He sees change as a complex, dilemma-ridden, technical, socio-political process which may appear simple but in reality is complex. Fullan's model has potential for those involved in the full actualization of the middle school concept as well as those focusing on the team process.

Despite the abundance of research on school improvement, there is little knowledge about *how* and *why* improvement occurs. Educators must realize that change is a process, not an event. Although more research is needed on *how* change occurs, it is obvious that individuals need to alter their ways of thinking and develop new skills for change to evolve.

The psychological elements of a successful change process include the following seven theses:

1. **Change takes place over time.** Change involves a number of factors that need to occur over a period of time. It is impossible for a school principal to mandate positive change. Sufficient lead time is needed to prepare a faculty for the transition to middle school or to implement team

teaching. Even though teachers may be organized into interdisciplinary teams, full implementation may take months or even years depending upon the degree to which the teachers are able to accept the teaming process as their mode for delivering instruction.

2. **The initial stages of any significant change always involve anxiety and uncertainty.** Teachers, students, parents, central office personnel, and school administrators are likely to be anxious about change. In planning for change, it is mandatory to deal with the affective issues of the change process. Although a factual base for the changes involved must be presented, there must also be adequate provision for people to release their apprehensions or anxieties. Those responsible for staff development programs must provide an opportunity for such a release in a developmental, accepting fashion.

3. **On-going technical assistance and psychological support assistance are crucial if the anxiety is to be coped with successfully.** Given the existence of anxiety as a reality, those responsible for program development must be able to train personnel in the skills required for success in instituting a new organizational system and also provide the necessary release for anxiety. Specific skills will be needed to help teachers function as members of a teaching team or develop and present a home base or teacher advisory program. Time must be allocated to learn the skills, but time must be available to respond to the apprehensions of those receiving the technical assistance. The total inservice process must include both cognitive information and a release for anxieties.

4. **Change involves learning new skills through practice and feedback; it is incremental and developmental.** The technical assistance described must be presented to teachers, school administrators, and central office personnel using appropriate teaching techniques for adult learners. The learning process includes practice and feedback that reflect the concepts of mentoring and follow-up beyond the initial presentation. Staff development sessions must subdivide the content into sequential portions that reflect developmental learning for experienced professionals learning a new approach.

5. **The most fundamental breakthrough occurs when people can cognitively understand the underlying conception and rationale with the respect to "why this new way works better."** Inservice training must provide an opportunity for teachers to cognitively comprehend the psychology of the early adolescent learner, the rationale for middle level curriculum, the organizational options for these grades, and the team process. The motivation for these sessions must include and support why the proposed approaches better meet the needs of the early adolescent learner. Teachers are more likely to implement change when they fully understand and can witness for themselves why the change is better for the student.

6. **Organizational conditions make it more or less likely that the process will succeed.** Administrative leadership, both in the central office as well as the local school, is extremely important for change to occur. Administrative personnel need to believe in these changes before they can expect teachers to implement them. Teachers will look at administrators as role models in this change process. Administrative personnel must make a commitment to understanding the middle school concept thoroughly before expecting staff members to do the same. The master schedule must help to create an environment in which various aspects of the team process can grow and develop; thus, the creation of the master schedule is an essential early step.

7. **Successful change involves pressure through interaction with peers as well as administrative leaders.** Those teachers who are not fully committed to the team concept will need to feel pressure from others who are enthusiastic about the program. The peer pressure of those opposed to the change could deter the success of the change process if left unchecked. Administrators must work hard to insure that peer pressure is positive, supportive, understanding, and nurturing.

WHAT IS STAFF DEVELOPMENT?

Staff development is the means by which professionals in a school district learn how to implement new methods and grow professionally. As new programs emerge nationally or locally, teachers need to learn how to implement these concepts. Central office as well as local school administrators should provide teachers with intense periods of study so they will understand these innovations.

When teachers know about a new program, they are better able to contribute to its design. When they contribute to the design of the program, they feel more responsible for its success. When teachers feel more responsible for the success of the program, these programs are more successful.

School districts cannot turn to undergraduate schools to provide the needed cadre of teachers for newer programs nor can they depend on graduate programs to provide the needed training. Therefore, school districts have to provide teachers opportunities to grow professionally on the job via a variety of professional improvement programs.

Staff development is more critical at the middle level because of rapid growth in the number of schools adopting the middle school concept and the lack of appropriately prepared teachers. Without staff development, change has little chance to occur. Successful staff development activities involve teachers in decision making, goal-setting, leadership activities, and an assessment of the process. Motivation and interest must be sustained by those responsible for staff development within the school or district. The ultimate goal is faculty support through intrinsic motivation. The principal plays a major leadership role but needs to encourage leadership to emerge from the faculty. Finding ways to actively involve the faculty in all aspects of staff development enhances the probability of successful program implementation.

CHARACTERISTICS OF AN EFFECTIVE STAFF DEVELOPMENT PROGRAM

A successful staff development program at the middle level must be based on adult learning theory. Adults are the ones changing from one form of school organization to another. A major outcome is a change in the pattern of meanings, values, behaviors, and attitudes of teachers. Participants in staff development programs must realize the need for change and be able to integrate the needed changes into their daily operating habits.

For adults, change is particularly complex because it involves the elimination of old patterns as well as the implementation of new ones. There is a definite risk of failure for adults participating in a staff development experience. Although those who attend these activities want to learn something new, they are fearful that they will be less successful in the future than in the past when less complex systems were in place. Self-concept is as important an issue for adult learners as it is for early adolescents.

Feinman (1980) points out that adult learning experiences should be "minds on" as well as "hands on." Adult learners must learn how to learn from their own experiences. This process is called reflective analysis and involves bringing new meanings and relationships to a level of conscious awareness. New learning should be applied in real life situations.

Those responsible for staff development should plan activities that focus on the individual and are problem oriented. Wherever possible, adults should draw on their own experiences. They should study theory and research, observe demonstrations, and practice with feedback. Coaching for successful transfer and application as well as peer support groups are other key ingredients.

A successful staff development program at the middle level must recognize the importance of the twelve factors or conditions described briefly below.

1. A thorough understanding of the middle school concept
The staff development program must enable administrators, teachers, parents, and the community to know what a middle school is, how the middle level program can and should respond to the needs of early adolescents, what school organizational options are, and how to help teachers work as members of a teaching team. With an understanding of these basics, the staff development program will help teachers achieve the real potential of the middle school concept.

2. Definite goals, objectives, and an organizational plan

There needs to be a master plan for the implementation of the team process that will enable those responsible to translate theory into practice. Definite goals and objectives are needed to guide the program. These can be re-evaluated at certain key points along the way as activities are assessed in relationship to goals pursued. Each facet of the organizational plan should fit in with the overall scheme. The curriculum for staff development must be meshed with learner objectives. Coaching should be used to insure successful transfer. The goals should meet individual needs and lead toward modified teacher behavior.

3. Sufficient lead time prior to the implementation of the project

Ideally, a staff development program should begin a minimum of one year before the conversion to middle school or implementation of a new program to allow sufficient time for program development and orientation activities. Many school districts have utilized two full years of preparation so that teachers, parents, students, and members of the community could be more deeply involved in the transition process.

4. A sustained, sequential, continuous effort

Staff development cannot consist of one inservice course prior to the opening of school, one workshop lead by an outside consultant, or one speech given by the president of the state organization for middle level schools. Each of these activities may be desirable, but staff development should provide a variety of activities on a continuous basis. Additional activities should be based upon an evaluation of earlier activities. Follow-up is essential.

5. A sensitivity to the needs of teachers

Just as classroom instruction should be based on needs of students, staff development should be based on the needs of the participants. A formal assessment process may be utilized to identify those needs. Once needs are identified, appropriate and meaningful programs can be planned based on those needs as well as adult learning theory. A variety of resources should be utilized, and activities should be problem oriented. Peer support systems should be monitored for effectiveness. Programs can be modified according to feedback received from participants. Again, the goal is to modify teacher behavior.

6. Motivate participants

Participants must be confident that they can meet the challenge of the new program. While these individuals will benefit from staff development activities, they must function independently on a daily basis. Building on their own experiences and contributions, they will be doing something new that is perceived of as relevant and satisfying. Incentives should be provided for teachers to use concepts learned.

7. Learning environment should be positive, trusting, and safe

Those involved in staff development activities must feel secure as learners. The environment should be cooperative, not competitive. Activities should be presented in such a way as to respect the dignity of each individual. Their physical comfort is also important. Lighting, seating, temperature, visibility of slides or other visuals, and appropriate audio levels must be assessed regularly.

8. Active involvement of the participants

Participants should do more than view films and video tapes or listen to lectures. The staff development curriculum must reflect the importance of the participants' active involvement and feature a number of hands-on activities. The target audience should be involved in all levels of preparation, implementation, and evaluation. Participants should especially be involved in planning activities to match the inservice curriculum to the learners' objectives. Instructors should be aware of attention span limitations of the participants and provide examples whenever possible.

9. The provision to train new teachers assigned to the school

As new teachers are assigned to the school, provisions should be made to absorb them into the program and enable them to become contributing members of the faculty. Specific training modules should be designed for these novices. Instructors should promote transfer and application on a regular basis.

10. Strong leadership of the principal as well as leadership emerging from the faculty

Leadership is a shared responsibility between the principal and those participating in the staff development program. Strengths of various participants should be identified and utilized. Participants should feel administrative support throughout the learning process. Local resource personnel should be utilized where those individuals have demonstrated the necessary skills and expertise. At the district level, the emphasis is to achieve the successful implementation of the team approach to instruction in each building. At the local school level, the emphasis is to achieve a balanced implementation throughout the building.

11. Create a staff development resource center or a middle school resource center

Each district should have a center for staff development activities or a specific resource facility to enhance successful program implementation. Each individual school should also have a room or an area of the building where materials are available to teachers on a regular basis. In addition to print and non-print materials, the center also becomes the location for professional discussions.

12. The opportunity to add new dimensions to the program

Every aspect of the model program cannot be in place during the first year. Some components can be in place by year's end; other aspects will be developed over the next several years. Via the staff development program, participants will be able to contribute to the additions or refinements of the team teaching experience for students in that school or district. New aspects of the program should relate to assessed needs of students.

WHO IS RESPONSIBLE FOR THE STAFF DEVELOPMENT PROGRAM?

The school district has the ultimate responsibility for providing the necessary staff development for implementing team planning and teaching. The district determines the philosophy, rationale, and other guidelines. The implementation of the middle school concept should, in essence, be a fundamental part of the comprehensive staff development program of the district. In most cases, the district plans the total spectrum of staff development activities. Frequently, the staff development coordinator for the district outlines the role of the district and the role of the individual school.

Individual schools have a major responsibility in providing the staff development required in that building. In many ways, the principal serves as the head of the staff development program for that building. As the instructional leader of the school, the principal should be a key person in the areas of program implementation and staff development. The principal must have a general plan for staff development, work with the faculty to review goals, and monitor the implementation process. Additionally, the principal should be available to meet with groups of teachers, parents, central office personnel, or Board of Education members who need to ventilate their concerns, obtain support, or receive direction. The principal who can provide leadership, motivate staff members to actively contribute to the successful implementation of teaming, and handle the normal concerns that are raised is well on the road to developing an effective middle school program.

Teachers, of course, have a major stake in the success of the program. Some of the specific responsibilities of the faculty are to recognize the real potential of teaming, work within the framework of the teaching contract to meet the needs of pupils, offer constructive suggestions through appropriate channels, consider the needs of pupils in determining priorities of the program, and take advantage of opportunities for active involvement in developing the program.

Staff development is most effective when it is a shared responsibility between the school district and the individual school and, within the individual school, between the faculty and administration. The staff development coordinator for the district can work with an advisory committee that has both teachers and administrators as members of that committee. In this way, the program can be responsive to needs of the district as well as the needs of each middle school.

A PROCESS/CONTENT APPROACH TO STAFF DEVELOPMENT

A process/content approach is suggested for creating a staff development program. Process refers to techniques, procedures, or strategies used to achieve a goal or objective within the staff development program. Process implies a particular method of doing something such as an inservice course, a summer workshop, or visits to other middle schools. Content is simply defined as all of the subject matter or material contained in the staff development curriculum. Topics would usually include a study of the development of early adolescents, models for curriculum, and organizational options.

It is probably impossible to determine whether content or process is more important in assessing the value of the staff development program. Participants must be actively involved in a variety of meaningful activities. At the same time, they must have the opportunity to secure information or data underlying the concepts. In reality, it is the interaction of process and content that facilitates real learning on the part of those involved.

Some Examples of Process Activities

Examples of processes or staff development activities that are appropriate to use in implementing the middle school concept are highlighted below.

1. **Classroom observations and conferences.** As the principal and other members of the supervisory team observe teachers and hold individual conferences, they can assess the extent to which that teacher is implementing the program. This is an excellent time for a conference to help the teacher understand aspects of the program or feel good about the role that teacher is playing in making the new program work.

2. **Department meetings.** Disciplinary or single subject teams may use department meetings effectively for staff development purposes. Teachers involved in interdisciplinary teams also benefit from meeting with other teachers of the same subject.

3. **Team planning meetings.** Teaching teams — interdisciplinary, disciplinary, or core/combination — have an excellent opportunity for professional growth when they meet on a regular basis.

4. **Faculty meetings.** New ideas can be presented to the total faculty. Faculty meetings can be used for professional growth activities as well as administrative matters.

5. **Department chairmen meetings.** The principal can meet with department heads on a regular basis. Additionally, all of the department heads of a specific subject for the school district can meet periodically.

6. **Meetings with team leaders.** The principal should meet with team leaders in the school on a regular basis to insure good communication between teams and to exploit this group as a major policy recommending and faculty representation body.

7. **Meetings with teams.** The principal should meet periodically with each of the teams. These meetings provide the opportunity for the principal to see the personality of each team and to interact with individual teachers.

8. **Inservice courses.** Organized courses should be available for teachers and other staff members to participate in in-depth experiences relative to some aspect of middle level education..

9. **Attending conferences, conventions, institutes.** All professional personnel, especially teachers, benefit greatly by attending workshops and meetings that focus on middle grades education.

10. **Reading professional journals.** Schools should subscribe to journals, newsletters, and other services that provide up-to-date information about early adolescent students and programs. Such materials must be made readily available to faculty rather than kept in the principal's office or the library.

11. **Resource persons.** Experienced middle level educators can address a faculty or all of the teachers in a district about important aspects of middle level education. These sessions are usually motivational; staff members can identify with both professors and practitioners. Appropriate follow-up activities should follow.

12. **Teacher representation on committees.** At both the district and local school levels, there are opportunities to involve staff members in committees that address professional concerns. Some are standing committees; others may be formed just to look at a specific problem.

13. **Professional study days.** Workshops can be planned on days when students are not in school or are dismissed early so teachers can participate in staff development activities. Such days are usually built into the school calendar.

14. **Summer curriculum workshops.** Curriculum guides can be written and/or pilot projects can be developed by involving teachers and other staff members in summer workshops. This is also an excellent way to develop the leadership needed for the middle school to be successful.

15. **Graduate courses.** Colleges and universities offer courses that complement staff development programs. In many cases, teachers can be reimbursed for taking courses that extend their professional competencies.

16. **Visiting other schools.** Staff members can learn new information by visiting other middle schools that are in different stages of program implementation. Specific purposes should be established for these visits.

17. **Membership in professional organizations.** Professional growth occurs as a result of the activities and resources made available to members by professional organizations that focus on middle grades education.

18. **Mobile on-site training units.** A team of professionals can visit each school to teach teachers how to implement new programs and ideas. These teams can visit for several weeks during the school year.

19. **Mentoring.** Mentoring is a process in which an experienced member of the faculty takes a direct, personal interest in the professional development of younger staff members or teachers who were recently assigned to the building. The mentor becomes a role model to enable the protege to develop to maximum potential.

20. **Peer coaching.** In peer coaching, some teachers assume responsibility for the professional growth of their colleagues. The goal of coaching is to insure that the training received is being transferred to the classroom. To become a peer coach, one usually needs training in the related skills.

This list of processes for use in staff development is not exhaustive. Those responsible for staff development should think in terms of the tasks of implementing teaming as well as effective middle schools and how these tasks or activities can help to achieve that goal. These techniques should also be kept in mind while reading the next section on content.

Content Topics

A number of topics should comprise the content portion of the staff development program. Major topics are:

1. Characteristics of an Effective Middle School

2. Making the Transition to Middle School

3. The Early Adolescent Student
   A. Data about physical, intellectual, social-emotional, and moral development
   B. Implications for school organization, curriculum, role of the teacher, and nature of the learning environment

4. Drafting Key Documents
   A. Defining the Middle School
   B. Conducting a Needs Assessment
   C. Writing the Philosophy, Goals, and Rationale

5. Implementing a Curriculum Model
    A. Organized Knowledge
    B. Skills
    C. Personal Development

6. Organizational Options
    A. Interdisciplinary
    B. Disciplinary
    C. Combination

7. Role and Function of a Team

8. Team Building Activities

9. Articulation with Elementary and High Schools

10. Building the Master Schedule
    A. Block-of-Time Approach
    B. Steps in Constructing the Schedule
    C. Special Needs Students

11. Flexible/Modular Scheduling

12. Grouping and Regrouping Students for Instruction

13. Effective Use of Planning Periods

14. Resolving Conflicts Among Team Members

15. Teaching Strategies for Early Adolescents

16. Role of the Team Leader

17. Roles of Administrative/Supervisory Personnel

18. Evaluating the Program

Bringing Process and Content Together

The process and content factors need to be brought together at an appropriate point. For example, the content area may be "Teaching Strategies for Early Adolescents." Initially, it is necessary to differentiate an approach that may be taken at the district or local level. Secondly, it is helpful to identify processes that are intended to introduce the topic and other activities that will be used to reinforce the content or skills at some later stage. The introductory and reinforcement stages need to be carefully orchestrated. The following examples will illustrate how this may be done.

Content: "Teaching Strategies for Early Adolescents"

Level: School District

Introductory Process:
  Inservice courses
  Department chairmen meeting

Reinforcement Process:
  Meetings with teams
  Team planning meetings
  Classroom observations and conferences

Content: "Teaching Strategies for Early Adolescents"

Level: Local School

Introductory Process:
  Faculty meetings
  Guest speakers
  Department chairmen meetings

Reinforcement Process:
  Meetings with teams
  Team planning meetings
  Classroom observations and conferences

Content: "Role of the Team Leader"

Level: School District

Introductory:
  Summer workshop with consultant
  Faculty meeting

Reinforcement:
  Inservice course during fall semester
  Meetings of team leaders at individual schools
  Informal evaluation of team leader at the end of the first semester

Content: "Use of Flexible Scheduling Techniques"
Level: Local School
Introductory: Guest speaker on professional study day Faculty meeting - practicum experience for all faculty members
Reinforcement: Discussion at meetings of team leaders and the building principal Analysis of utilization of flexible scheduling practices conducted by the director of research

ESTABLISHING PRIORITIES AND TIMETABLE

A timeline should be developed for the purpose of introducing the team approach to instruction and identifying persons responsible for specific aspects of implementation. Priorities are needed; those involved should begin work immediately on those items essential at the outset of the process. The timetable then becomes a basis of evaluating the extent to which the program is being implemented.

The faculties of individual schools, the community, and central office personnel should have input in establishing priorities and determining the timetable. In this way, all who participate in programming the implementation can work cooperatively toward the goals which have been mutually established.

Priorities and a timetable are needed not only in the initial conversion to a middle school but also in the expansion of a program or the orientation of new staff members. Staff members should discuss such questions as:

1. What are our primary and secondary goals?

2. What are our immediate needs?

3. How can we adjust our list of priorities?

Dialogue and reflection on growth are needed in establishing priorities for the development of a timetable. Once developed, the timetable should be publicized to the community, taxpayers, parents, central office personnel, Board of Education members, and faculties. The timetable must be viewed, however, as subject to modification.

EVALUATING THE STAFF DEVELOPMENT PROGRAM

Consideration needs to be given to evaluating the staff development program. Johnston and Markle (1979) suggested a process of structured questioning or interviewing to reach valid and reliable conclusions about the effectiveness of a program. They suggest this list as a general scope and sequence for a question-directed evaluation.

1. What are we trying to evaluate? Precisely what portion of the total middle grades education package are we trying to assess? Program evaluation will be more effective if specific components of the program can be identified. For example, it is more desirable to define the object of evaluation as the "inservice courses" than the "staff development program" Or, the object of the evaluation can be "the use of the team planning period" rather than the "staff development program."

2. What do we expect this program component to accomplish? What are the specific objectives of the program? What do we expect teachers to do as a result of their participation in the program? For example, team planning periods might be expected to encourage teachers to focus more on the skill development processes as they plan their lessons. Also, team planning periods should help teachers focus more on the total learning needs of a student.

3. What will we accept as indicators that the program is achieving its objectives? Can we list the teacher behaviors that will allow us to conclude that the program element has had a desirable impact? Do teachers correlate topics in one subject with topics in other subjects? Do teachers on the team have a skill-of-the-week program?

4. What sources of data are available which will indicate the presence or absence of the indicators? What kinds of data on teacher behaviors do we already have? What kinds of data must be collected? Can structured observations of team activities be scheduled? Can teacher self-report data be utilized? In general, what kinds of data can be assessed in a reasonable period of time with a manageable effort?

5. What specific information from each source will be most valuable to the program evaluation? Within each data source, what information is most clearly related to the objectives of the program? How can this information be gathered, assembled, and organized?

6. What do the data that we have collected state about the indicators? Do the data state that the indicators are present or absent? What indicators are present that were not anticipated?

7. Based on the presence or absence of indicators, what can be concluded about the effectiveness of the program? Are the indicators of a process (inservice, team planning periods) present in sufficient numbers and strength to conclude that the program is working? Can the conclusion be justified on the basis of the data rather than personal opinion or the strength of one's desire for the program to succeed?

Although other approaches can be utilized, the model by Johnston and Markle can be used in assessing the effectiveness of elements of a staff development program.

SUMMARY

Staff development is the key to the successful implementation of teaming. Responsibility for staff development should be shared between the central office and the local school; however, principals play a major role in implementing new programs in their building. The interaction of process and content facilitates real learning on the part of those involved. Staff development enables teachers to make a significant contribution to the creation of a meaningful team experience.

Activity:

1. What is our staff development program for the middle grades?

2. What are the staff development needs of our teachers and staff?

3. How can we implement the process/content approach?

4. How will we evaluate our staff development program?

Epilogue

This book is designed to help classroom teachers implement the team process, an integral part of the middle school concept. The success of the middle school movement depends in large measure on the willingness and ability of teachers to implement the middle school concept in the classroom on a daily basis. Teachers can learn these techniques and strategies through staff development activities. A real commitment to utilize the various activities and strategies described in this book is needed if the middle school concept is to be fully achieved.

The team is the most important unit in the middle school organizational plan. Being a member of a team involves more than having a cognitive understanding of middle school literature. Team membership is very much an affective experience, demonstrating that adults can work together to best meet the developmental needs of early adolescents.

The team process is successful when. . .

- needs of students are met

- students feel good about themselves

- .the administration and school district support the teams' efforts

- block-of-time scheduling is utilized

- there is flexibility in daily, weekly, and monthly schedules

- teachers believe in the middle school concept

- special needs students are included within the team process

- conflicts among team members are resolved

- .team members are willing to share thoughts, ideas, and responsibilities

- organized knowledge and skill development are correlated regularly

- parents are integral to the team

- there is adequate time for team planning and that time is productive

- resource people are available to the team

- .the team leader successfully involves all members in team activities

- local options are utilized by the team

- pupils are in various grouping arrangements during the day

- team members practice good human relations skills

- teams take time to evaluate their effectiveness

- staff development activities are provided

Bibliography

Alexander, William et al. (1969) *The Emergent Middle School,* 2nd ed. New York: Holt, Rinehart and Winston, Inc.

Baltimore County (Maryland) Public Schools. (1983). *1984 and Beyond: A Reaffirmation of Values.* Towson, MD.

Baltimore County (Maryland) Public Schools. (1989). *Concept Paper on Least Restrictive Environment.* Towson, MD.

Baltimore County (Maryland) Public Schools. (1979). *Planning for Reading Instruction K-6.* Towson, MD.

Baltimore County (Maryland) Public Schools. (1983). *Question Power.* Towson, MD..

Baltimore County (Maryland) Public Schools. (1985). *Reading and Writing in the Middle School.* Towson, MD.

Benne, K., and Sheets, P. (1966). Functional Roles of Group Members. *Working with Groups,* 2nd ed, New York: John Wiley & Sons, Inc..

Brooks, Martin. (1986). "What is CLM?" *The CLM Journal:* II, No. 1.

Drash, Allan. (1975). "Variations in Pubertal Development and the School System: A Problem and a Challenge." *Transescence: The Journal On Emerging Adolescent Education.*, IV, 25.

Ehrenberg, Sydelle D. (1981). "Concept Learning: How to Make it Happen in the Classroom." *Educational Leadership,* 36:1, October, pp. 36-43.

Eichhorn, Donald. (1973). "The Boyce Medical Study." *Educational Dimensions of the Emerging Adolescent Learner,* N. Atkins and P. Pumerantz (EDS.),. Washington: ASCD and Educational Leadership Institute.

Epstein, Herman T. and Toepfer, Conrad, Jr. (1978). "A Neuroscience Basis for Reorganizing Middle School Education." *Educational Leadership:* 36:8 May.

Farel, Anita M. (1982). *Early Adolescence: What Parents Need to Know.* University of North Carolina at Chapel Hill: The Center for Early Adolescence.

Feinman, S. and Floder, R. (1980). "A Consumer's Guide to Teacher Development." *Journal of Staff Development*, 1:2, pp. 126-147.

Fullan, Michael. (1985). "Change Processes and Strategies at the Local Level." *The Elementary School Journal*, 85:5, pp. 395-421.

Fullmer, Daniel and Bernard, Harold. (1968). *Counseling: Content and Process*. Chicago: Science Research Associates.

Fusco, Esther and Associates. (1987). *Cognitive Matched Instruction in Action*. Columbus: National Middle School Association.

Gay, Geneva. (1978). "Ethnic Identification in Early Adolescence: Some Implications for Instructional Reform." *Educational Leadership*: 35, May, pp. 649-655.

Johnston, J. Howard and Markle, Glenn (1979). "Evaluating Programs for Young Adolescents: An Unconventional Approach." *Transescence: The Journal on Emerging Adolescent Education*, VII, pp. 13-16.

Kohlberg, Lawrence. (1973). *Collected Papers on Moral Development and Moral Education*. Cambridge: Harvard University Laboratory for Human Development.

Lomax, R. G. and Cooley, W. W. (1980). "The Student Achievement Instructional Time Relationship." Paper presented at the Annual Meeting of the American Educational Research Association, Boston, MA.

Merenbloom, Elliot Y. (1988). *Developing Effective Middle Schools Through Faculty Participation*. Columbus: National Middle School Association.

Merenbloom, Elliot Y. (1981). "Implementing Team Teaching: Three Models." *Dissemination Services on the Middle Grades*, XII, March.

O'Neil, John. (1988). "The `Regular Education Initiative': Seeking Integration Between Special, Regular Education." *ASCD Curriculum Update*, September, pp. 4-6.

Purkey, William. (1978). *Inviting School Success: A Self-Concept Approach to Teaching and Learning*. Belmont: Wadsworth Publishing.

Shertzer, Bruce and Stone, Shelley C. (1966). *Fundamentals of Guidance*. Boston: Houghton Mifflin.

Shockley, Robert and Johnston, J. Howard. (1983) "Time on Task: Implications for Middle Level Instruction." *Schools in the Middle*. National Association of Secondary School Principals, December.

Steer, Donald (Ed.). (1980). *The Emerging Adolescent: Characteristics and Educational Implications*. Columbus: National Middle School Association.

Sund, Robert B. (1976). *Piaget for Educators*. Columbus: Charles E. Merril Publishing.

Thornburg, Hershel. (1974). *Preadolescent Development: Readings*. Tucson: University of Arizona Press.

Thornburg, Hershel. (1979). *The Bubblegum Years: Sticking With Kids From 9-13*. Tucson: Help Books.

Tobin, Kenneth G. (1980). "The Effect of an Extended Teacher Wait-Time on Science Achievement." *Journal of Research in Science Teaching*, No.17, pp. 469-475.

Tobin, Kenneth G. and Capie, William (1981). "Wait-Time in Science." *The Middle-Junior High Science Bulletin*, V, No.1, Fall.

Toepfer, Conrad F., Jr. (1979). "Inservice Needs in the Middle Grades." *Dissemination Services on the Middle Grades*, XI, November, pp. 1-14.

Toepfer, Conrad F., Jr. (1979). "Areas for Further Investigation Suggested by Brain Growth Periodization Findings." *Transesence: The Journal on Emerging Adolescent Education*, VII, pp. 17-20.

Traxler, Arthur E. and North, Robert D. (1966). *Techniques of Guidance*. New York: Harper and Row.

Index

Publications

NATIONAL MIDDLE SCHOOL ASSOCIATION

How to Evaluate Your Middle School, Sandra L. Schurr (86 pages)

Connecting the Curriculum Through Interdisciplinary Instruction, John H. Lounsbury, Editor (168 pages)

Nurturing a Teacher Advisory Program, Claire Cole (54 pages)

Involving Families in Middle Level Education, John Myers, Luetta Monson (56 pages)

This We Believe, National Middle School Association (40 pages)

The ABC's of Evaluation—26 Alternative Ways to Assess Student Progress, Sandra Schurr (232 pages)

Treasure Chest, Cheryl Hoversten, Nancy Doda, John Lounsbury (268 pages)

Homework: A New Direction, Neila A. Connors (104 pages)

Professional Preparation and Certification, National Middle School Association (24 pages)

On Site: Preparing Middle Level Teachers Through Field Experiences, Deborah A. Butler, Mary A. Davies, and Thomas S. Dickinson (84 pages)

As I See It, John H. Lounsbury (112 pages)

The Team Process: A Handbook for Teachers, Third and enlarged edition, Elliot Y. Merenbloom (173 pages)

Life Stories: The Struggle for Freedom and Equality in America, Lynn L. Mortensen, Editor (166 pages)

Education in the Middle Grades: Overview of National Practices and Trends, Joyce L. Epstein and Douglas J. Mac Iver (92 pages)

Middle Level Programs and Practices in the K-8 Elementary School: Report of a National Study, C. Kenneth McEwin and William M. Alexander (46 pages)

A Middle School Curriculum: From Rhetoric to Reality, James A. Beane (84 pages)

Visions of Teaching and Learning: Eighty Exemplary Middle Level Projects, John Arnold, Editor (160 pages)

The New American Family and the School, J. Howard Johnston (48 pages)

The Japanese Junior High School: A View from the Inside, Paul S. George (56 pages)

Schools in the Middle: Status and Progress, William M. Alexander and C. Kenneth McEwin (112 pages)

A Journey Through Time: A Chronology of Middle Level Resources, Edward J. Lawton (36 pages)

Dynamite in the Classroom: A How-To Handbook for Teachers, Sandra L. Schurr (272 pages)

Developing Effective Middle Schools Through Faculty Participation, Second and enlarged Edition, Elliot Y. Merenbloom (122 pages)

Preparing to Teach in Middle Level Schools, William M. Alexander and C. Kenneth McEwin (64 pages)

Guidance in Middle Level Schools: Everyone's Responsibility, Claire Cole (31 pages)

Young Adolescent Development and School Practices: Promoting Harmony, John Van Hoose and David Strahan (68 pages)

When the Kids Come First: Enhancing Self-Esteem, James A. Beane and Richard P. Lipka (96 pages)

Interdisiciplinary Teaching: Why and How, Gordon F. Vars (56 pages)

The Middle School, Donald H. Eichhorn (128 pages)

Positive Discipline: A Pocketful of Ideas, William Purkey and David Strahan (56 pages)

Teachers as Inquirers: Strategies for Learning With and About Early Adolescents, Chris Stevenson (52 pages)

Adviser-Advisee Programs: Why, What, and How, Michael James (75 pages)

Evidence for the Middle School, Paul George and Lynn Oldaker (52 pages)

Involving Families in Middle Level Education, John W. Myers (52 pages)

Perspectives: Middle Level Education, John H. Lounsbury, Editor (190 pages)

To order, please phone NMSA with a VISA or MasterCard number or send your order with check, money order, or purchase order to NMSA.

National Middle School Association
2600 Corporate Exchange Dr., Ste. 370
Columbus, OH 43231
800-528-NMSA